Published by
Vitasta Publishing Pvt Ltd
2/15, Ansari Road, Daryaganj
New Delhi-110 002
info@vitastapublishing.com

ISBN 978-93-90961-33-7

First Edition 2022

MRP ₹595

Edited by Veena Batra
Cover and layout by Somesh Kumar Mishra
Printed by Chaman Enterprises, New Delhi

PRAFULL
GORADIA

Banaras to Jerusalem
AND OTHER ESSAYS

Vitasta
LET KNOWLEDGE SPREAD

Contents

Banaras to Jerusalem

IT IS IRONIC that this sacred city, whose name originates from the ancient Yerushalayim meaning 'city of peace', should have been invaded forty times, destroyed twice and yet has lived on since time immemorial. Notwithstanding that Jerusalem is the spiritual cradle of all the three religions, yet more blood of war has flowed in its alleys than in any other holy city. Jews have been butchered again and again particularly by Christians. In turn, the worshippers of Jesus have been killed by Muslims, while the followers of Allah have been slaughtered by Jews and Christians.

Yet unquestionably Jerusalem is blessed by divinity. When we visited it, I was feeling as weak as a kitten and to walk even a hundred yards was difficult. The four of us–my wife Nayana, my cousin Dilip, his wife Jyoti and I went to the market at the foot of the Calvary Hill on a fine morning. Where the line of shops ended I sat down and told everyone that maybe I would go with them up to station two. There I would sit and wait until they returned from the top of the hill. I do not know what happened to me that I climbed on and on with the other three. I climbed to the fourteenth station to visit the Church of Sepulchre where Jesus was buried and we came down together. What the power was that drew me to climb, I could not say; I am not a Christian.

Judaism was born in a way on Mount Sinai where God Jehovah announced his eternal Ten Commandments to Prophet Moses. Jesus Christ performed many of His miracles as well as shared his wisdom with the people in and around Jerusalem.

What is the mystery behind so much violence in so sacred a city? The Philistine giant led his men to the north of Jerusalem. Saul, the leader of the defending people, the Israelites, was taken aback and was at a loss of what to do. Young David, a local standing nearby suddenly took a sling shot and the stone pierced the giant Goliath's forehead to kill him. The Israelites were overjoyed and King Saul anointed David as his successor. This is as stated in the Bible. David is looked upon as the first effective King of Judea. He was succeeded by his son Solomon (born to his wife Bathsheba), who built the legendary Temple on the Mount. This was some years before 1000 BC.

Decades passed until well-known King Nebuchadnezzar of Babylon invaded Judea, laid siege to Jerusalem and eventually destroyed the city by setting fire to it. Of the citizens surviving the siege, 20,000 were dispatched to Babylon. The Temple, so dear to those who subsequently came to be called Jews, was destroyed. Between those killed and exiled, ten of the twelve tribes perished and today's Jews belong to the surviving two. All in all, the devastation was unspeakable, if not also unthinkable. When the Persian emperor Artaxerxes heard of all this, he was disturbed because his father lay buried in Jerusalem. He had a local potentate rebuild the walls around the city of David and the Temple Mount. Jerusalem prospered after this episode of horror.

The history of this city of Prophet Abraham, the father of religions of the Western world, was thus studded with more and more violence. Yet these highly-educated people, whether in Europe or North America recognise Jerusalem as their holiest destination of pilgrimage. And I, who am neither a Westerner nor educated in the West, experienced the pull of the supernatural. Can anything explain this phenomenal paradox?

The three religions spawned by Prophet Abraham have a single exclusive god; Jehovah (Jews), son of god Jesus (Christians) and Allah (Muslims). They have one prophet each to whom they give their total allegiance–Moses, Jesus Christ and Muhammad respectively. They have a book each—the Torah, Bible and the Quran whom the believers must not question. All three religions expect their followers to await doomsday or *qayamat*, whenever it comes, whether the believer is alive or in his or her grave. Jews, Christians and Muslims are religious cousins, if not siblings. They are in Arabic Ahl-e-Kitab or people of the Book. Yet possibly, no other communities have fought so much and killed so many of their religious siblings as the followers of Abraham? Why?

Conceptually, I hasten to submit that their theologies are victims of the Deductive Logic they have followed whose reasoning begins with a firm and clear premise that my God is the best and there is no other god. Islam says no one can reach heaven or *jannat* unless he is a Muslim. There are no spiritual opportunities beyond the precise notion of Jehovah, Christ and Allah. The maximum the Muslims have been able to venture into is Sufism. The intelligent believer in any of these three religions can feel stifled. The unthinking one enjoys the precise readymade prescription of how to live, to worship and to do what and when. With the progress of education, more and more people have taken to thinking. They wonder whether they should swallow wholesale the legends and fables they are told. The assertion that there is such and such a god, without conducting a survey, celestial or earthly, can become difficult for the odd enlightened person. In short, for those who can readily accept the premise, all the three religions and their scriptures are consistent, not difficult to follow and are helpful in leading a good life.

In contrast, Hinduism has one or two essentials–faith in one's karma and its reaction good or bad. Secondly, transmigration of souls: life, death, again life, death, on and on until the excellence of one's karma releases a particular soul from rebirth… For the rest, a Hindu can believe in what he likes, including non-believing and being an agnostic. There is no question of being condemned as an apostate.

Judaism has over the centuries lost quite a number of its followers although a large number have been killed in pogroms and exterminations. Christianity has allowed itself to be split into many denominations whenever its followers have had serious differences of opinion. Islam has discouraged rethinking and has practised *taqlid* (orthodoxy) for the last thousand years. It has discouraged the advanced education of women and has thus tried to shut out questioning and debate. If a Muslim leaves his religion he is declared a *murtad* or an apostate who can by a *fatwa* be punished to death.

A Hindu, with his inductive logic feels his mission fulfilled if he is happy with his karma performed or which he is performing whether for his family, caste or society in general. Whereas, an Abrahamic has to serve his society and perform well so that on doomsday, he may hope to be sent to heaven. Some Abrahamics might do some social service in the cause of their people or serve the people through political governance. What about the others? Some feel they can serve their country by fighting for its cause, which would generally be dominated by religion; hence, the frequent fighting and wars.

As the first millennium turned and the first century of the last millennium before Christ came, the fortunes of Jerusalem again turned foul. The Jews were divided into three factions. One wanted the Romans on some terms, the second desired settlement and the third peace at any cost. Disunity is the surest path to defeat. So it happened at the hands of Titus, the Roman Emperor's son, who laid waste the holy city. The second time the temple was destroyed and has not been rebuilt yet. After three years of bitter fighting when there was no hope left other than slavery, their leader said to the survivors: "My generous friends, we resolved long ago never to be servants to the Romans nor to any other than God Himself. We were the first that revolted against them; we are the last that fight against them and I cannot but esteem it as a favour that God has granted us that it is still in our power to die bravely and in a state of freedom, in a glorious manner, together with our dearest friends. Let our wives die before they are abused and our children before they have tasted slavery".

So the "husbands tenderly embraced their wives, and took their children into their arms, giving the longest parting kisses to them with tears in their eyes". Each man killed his wife and children; ten men were chosen to slay the rest until all 960 were dead.

Jerusalem was invaded by any number of kings, ranging from the Greeks to Napoleon Bonaparte in 1799, to the German Kaiser Wilhelm in 1898. Some were helpful, others indifferent and yet others utterly destructive. What was their attraction for coming? Must have been god and religion, but then why destroy? There was no big wealth to loot either. The Russians came with a clear intention to settle down as Jews were being expelled by the Czars from time to time. According to Sir Moses Montefiore (president of Board of British Jews), two million Jews left Russia between 1888 and 1914. The majority went to the USA but a large number came to Jerusalem.

The remarkable turning point in the future of the city was the repeated visits, six in all, of the wealthy old man Sir Moses Montefiore, who once even dreamed of buying Jerusalem. But other wealthy Jews in England like the Rothschilds did not think it was a sensible idea. Nevertheless, he set up a number of welfare schemes for the local Jews. The shining example was his establishing the 'Montefiore Quarter'.

If there be any other city on earth that can be called Jerusalem's sibling in divine status, historical antiquity, religious significance and also a saga of suffering, it has to be Banaras in India, known as Kashi and also Varanasi, both ancient names of the city. The holiest of the seven Hindu holy cities of Kashi, Mathura, Dwarka, Kanchi (Kanchipuram), Haridwar, Ujjain and Ayodhya, Banaras is central not only to the Hindu religion, but to Hindu society and its ethos itself. The city's name Varanasi is a combination of the names of two tributaries of the Ganga forming the city's borders: Varuna, flowing in northern Varanasi, and Assi, a smaller stream in the southern part of the city, near Assi Ghat. The ancient part of the city is located on the northern shores of the Ganges, bounded by Varuna and Assi. Kashi was one of the sixteen *mahajanapadas* (great states) that existed and flourished in ancient India. Kashi, though, differs from its West Asian sibling in one major respect. The kingdom of Kashi *janapada* was bigger than the city of Varanasi. Jerusalem in contrast has stood alone as a "shining city on the hill".

The *Rigveda* since the Vedic times refers to Kasi (Kashi) which in Sanskrit means "that which lightens up", making Banaras the "City of Light", or the "luminous city as an eminent seat of learning". The name has been in continuous use by pilgrims, travellers and Hindus in general. Since time immemorial, Banaras has been a place of learning and enlightenment signified most notably in the modern age by the Banaras Hindu University (BHU), founded by Pandit Madan Mohan Malviya, a highly-learned scholar, Congress leader, a contemporary of Mahatma Gandhi and a freedom fighter during India's independence movement. Believing Hindus hold that death and cremation in Banaras are a guarantee of *moksha* (salvation), i.e., complete deliverance from the cycle of birth, death and rebirth. The holy city is believed to have been founded by Lord Shiva himself. Shiva, who is also known as Mahakala or the entity above even Death and Dissolution, as Banaras' presiding deity, signifies the timelessness of the city.

Dashashwamedh Ghat, on the banks of the Ganga in Banaras, is indelibly etched in the minds of those who have visited it even once. Emperors and kings have come and gone, empires have risen and fallen, yet the faithful have thronged here for many millennia to walk down the steps and bow their heads to God Almighty and the Ganga, which emanates from His feet. She is reverently called Gangaji. It is said that it was here at this very site that the King of Kashi or, as some others believe Brahma the Creator Himself, dedicated ten (*dasha)* horses in an Ashwamedha *yajna*; hence the name Dashashwamedh. People believe that those who bathe in the river on this ghat are showered with blessings, which emanate from that Ashwamedha *yajna* thousands of years ago.

Banaras, the abode of both mortal passing and salvation and steeped in legend, was not created or shaped by political power or military conquest, unlike Jerusalem. It has been driven by faith and the esoteric power of the metaphysical realm. So deep is the faith of the devout that millions of pilgrims converge here, from every corner of the Indian subcontinent since many millennia.

How old is Banaras? Possibly, even time may not have an answer to that. About Kashi's antiquity, Mark Twain had this to say: "Varanasi is older than history, older than tradition, and older than legend; and twice as old as all of them put together". The number of temples and shrines dedicated to Shiva in Varanasi are too numerous to be mentioned, with Vishweshwar or Kashi Vishwanath the most prominent, and among the twelve *jyotirlingas* of Shiva. The city has been mentioned by Rama himself in the Ramayana. It has association with Krishna too and the events of the Mahabharata; Bhishma, the grand old man of the Kuru Dynasty abducted the three princesses of Kashi to get them married into the Kuru clan. Years later, the Pandavas visited the city to atone for their sin of fratricide committed in the Great Kurukshetra War. Kashi's monarch, a mighty warrior, joined the Pandava side in that war, and fought and fell while protecting Pandava ruler Yudhishthira on the twelfth day of the war. Perhaps this was apt for Varanasi, whose rulers since the days of yore, enjoined by tradition, have been the upholders of dharma. Yudhishthira was famed as Dharmaraj, i.e., the very embodiment of dharma and it was befitting that the king of Kashi, a protector of dharma should attain a heroic death in his defence.

Banaras is where Gautama Buddha preached his first sermon in the city's famed deer park, after he attained enlightenment and became the Buddha. It can be rightly called the founding place of Buddhism. While Banaras accommodated the new faith, it refused to be swept away by it. Kashi, the centre of Vedic learning, remained unconquered, even as Buddhism appeared to be on a relentless victorious march everywhere else. The Jataka tales, which describe the Buddha's incarnations in his previous lives before appearing on earth as the Buddha, clearly indicate that Varanasi was one of the richest cities in all of India, famed for its prosperity and opulence. When the Buddha passed from the mortal world, it is said that his remains were wrapped in cotton cloth woven in Kashi. The city is also where Adi Shankara began his *dharmic* reconquest of India to resuscitate Hinduism. Goswami Tulsidas' seminal *Ramcharitmanas*, which led to the revival of Hinduism in the Mughal era, was written by the saint-poet on the banks of the Ganga in Varanasi. The Banaras *gharana* (tradition) among the *gharanas* of Indian classical music remains one of its most dominant.

And like Jerusalem, Banaras has seen and endured invasion, desecration and agony too. Nowhere is this more evident than the Gyan Vapi semi-mosque, which is actually the site where the original Kashi Vishwanath temple stood. Gyan Vapi literally means the Well of Knowledge, and the ancient temple was targeted for destruction by the iconoclastic Mughal emperor Aurangzeb (1658-1707), whose hatred for infidel Hindus and their religion was visceral. Demolished under the Mughal ruler's orders in 1669, the erstwhile temple's plinth was left largely untouched and continued to serve as the courtyard of the mosque, clearly to remind Hindus of their humiliation. The southern wall (along with its cusped arches and exterior mouldings) was also spared and turned into the *qibla* wall of the semi-mosque built on the demolished part. The desecration can move even the non-devout to pathos. There are innumerable other ancient temples in the city that have suffered a similar fate.

But Banaras has stood resolute and unyielding even in the darkest period of jihadi barbarism. The rulers of Banaras in the 18th century began to reassert their freedom, strengthening the kingdom both westwards towards Jaunpur and Awadh and eastwards towards the present-day Gorakhpur, Basti, Deoria, Azamgarh, Ballia, Bihar and even up to the fringes of Bengal. These medieval Hindu rulers of Banaras were mostly from the Bhumihar caste, and would not hesitate to clash with the Mughals and later the East India Company. Bound by a strong sense of clan, the rajas of Banaras in the mid-1700s could often raise an army of more than 100,000 men to defend Banaras as well as the Hindu way of life. The East India Company after its victory at Plassey (Palashi) in 1757 worsted the Mughal Emperor Shah Alam-II in the Battle of Buxar in 1764 to acquire the *diwani* (revenue collection) rights of all of Bengal and Bihar, but faced a torrid battle in trying to overcome the then raja of Banaras, Chet Singh. Banaras under his leadership first drove out its rival the Nawab of Awadh and later also forced the then Governor General Warren Hastings to beat a retreat to Chunar. One of the city's ghats is named in honour of Raja Chet Singh.

Like Ayodhya, Mathura and innumerable other Hindu temples demolished by medieval Islamic rulers, Hindus have neither forgotten nor relinquished their right to this holiest of their religious places. The desecrated site (especially the plinth) became an even more popular hub for Hindus from all over the country. Ayodhya has been reclaimed after a five-century battle; like Jerusalem, Banaras awaits its liberation from historical injustice.

Why Jews Remained Homeless Until 1948

IT IS A mystery why the resourceful Jewish community did not get down to acquiring or organising a territory to stay on, pending the acquisition of their original homeland, which was Judea. As is well known, the Zionist mission was to obtain this homeland, inclusive of Jerusalem. In 1917, Britain's then Foreign Secretary Lord Arthur Balfour issued a declaration announcing support for the establishment of a national home for the Jewish people in Palestine, famous as the Balfour Declaration. Yet, it took 31 years before the state of Israel could be achieved. Thereafter also, the Israelis have displayed enormous resourcefulness in expanding their state on the Golan Heights in Syria, parts of the West Bank of the Jordan River and, of course, the eastern half of Jerusalem despite fighting three wars with the Arabs in 1956, 1967 and 1973. They have signed peace treaties with Egypt and Jordan, and have recently established diplomatic ties with Bahrain, the UAE and Qatar, and developed friendly ties with none other than Saudi Arabia.

Anti-semitism and the persecution of the Jews, including periodical pogroms, began soon after the monarchies in Europe established themselves on their thrones. In other words, the entire community was a target of persecution from the 6th century AD. In due course, the occupational opportunities for them were confined to moneylending, trading and practising as doctors and lawyers. The 19th century onwards, Jews gradually began to emigrate to the USA, where there was no persecution, although implicit prejudice could not be ruled out.

On the other hand, the Jewish community as a whole was wealthy. The Rothschild family are prominent bankers in many European countries. Germany was reputed to have perhaps the largest Jewish community. The Nazi party was established more or less on the morrow of the end of World War I. Adolf Hitler and his anti-semites were known across the country by 1923. His manifesto called *Mein Kampf*, spewing hatred against the Jews as well as the Slavs, was published soon thereafter.

By January 1933, Hitler had become Chancellor of Germany. In any case, whether before or after coming to power, seldom were his speeches free of spewing venom against the Jews. On 9 and 10 November 1938 was perpetrated virtually a national pogrom.

Kristallnacht or the Night of Broken Glass, also called the November Pogrom(s) was a violent attack against Jews carried out by the Nazis' Sturmabteilung (Storm Detachment) paramilitary forces and civilians throughout Nazi Germany on 9-10 November 1938. The German authorities looked on without intervening. The name *Kristallnacht* (Crystal Night) comes from the shards of broken glass that littered the streets after the windows of Jewish-owned stores, buildings and synagogues were smashed. The pretext for the attacks was the assassination of the German diplomat Ernst von Rath by Herschel Grynszpan, a 17-year-old German-born Polish Jew living in Paris.

Jewish homes, hospitals and schools were ransacked as attackers demolished buildings with sledgehammers. Rioters destroyed 267 synagogues throughout Germany, Austria and the Sudetenland. Over 7,000 Jewish businesses were damaged or destroyed, and 30,000 Jewish men were arrested and incarcerated in concentration camps. British historian Martin Gilbert wrote that no event in the history of German Jews between 1933 and 1945 was so widely reported as it was happening, and the accounts from foreign journalists working in Germany sent shockwaves around the world. *The Times* of London observed on 11 November 1938: "No foreign propagandist bent upon blackening Germany before the world could outdo the tale of burnings and beatings, of blackguardly assaults on defenceless and innocent people, which disgraced that country yesterday".

Jews across Europe were aware of these events in Germany and wanted to escape by emigrating. But emigrate to where was the question? Almost all countries refused entry to them and ships carrying Jewish refugees were mostly turned back even in Palestine. By the 1930s, the local Arabs were apprehensive of being eventually outnumbered by the Jews. But due to some strange reasoning, for twelve centuries the Jews had remained complacent regarding hiring, leasing or purchasing a homeland of their own while waiting for Judea, regarding which there was no definite promise in the declaration of 1917. Surely, until before petroleum was discovered in some place or the other in

Arabia, territory would have been available.

In early 20th century, before WWI, the Russian Czarist Empire was land-rich but money-poor. During that war, quite often, three Russian soldiers fought with one rifle. Earlier, the Czar had sold Alaska to the USA. This region comprises nearly 600,000 square miles. It was sold for a sum of 72 lakh dollars. Libya, as another example has 6,80,000 square miles and a population of less than 66 lakhs, meaning plenty of land. Moreover, Libya is not from Judea and pre-petroleum it had a poor economy. In fact, the peninsula was a desert area with some Bedouins on camels. In the years between the two world wars, the Sheikh of Kuwait used to visit Mumbai every year during the monsoon and stay in a guesthouse near the Mumba Devi Temple at only Rs 2 per night without food. Today Kuwait enjoys one of the highest per capita incomes in the world.

Hebrew or Jewish history begins sketchily in the Greek or Hellenic times, about 3,500 years ago. The people of Moses endured centuries of captivity and virtual slavery. Thereafter also, their history is a catalogue of oppression, anti-semitism and suffering most of the time at most of the places they lived. The golden time they enjoyed was in Islamic Spain between the 8th and 14th centuries. Their stay in the early Ottoman Empire between the 14th and 16th centuries was happy, as it was in Poland until the beginning of World War II in September 1939. The USA has treated them well during the last century. The comparatively limited members who settled in India and lived for centuries were comprehensively happy and socially assimilated. As one Jewish eminence visiting from Israel said: "The Hindus have never made us weep. If our people had tears in their eyes, the Hindus promptly wiped them". For the rest, the Jews have suffered socially dark lives. Yet no Jewish leader thought of acquiring a land or country of their own even temporarily. I wonder why?

For the believing Jews, their religion was above all, above the country of residence. They were supra-nationalist and craved for their homeland in Judea. The contention here is why they tolerated killing and other suffering, including pogroms, which all climaxed with the holocaust during World War II.

The Jews are a clever and capable people and they have produced a substantial number of Nobel Laureates in a variety of spheres. How can we believe that they did not think of a temporary land en route to the homeland in Judea which they eventually obtained in 1948?

Indic Voice

WHY ONLY THE United Nations, even scholars in the West do not know the fundamental difference between the Abrahamic religions and the Eastern faiths, especially Hinduism. True, Swami Vivekananda had made a marvellous start at the Parliament of Religions at Chicago in 1893 and followed it up in the short life left to him. Thereafter, however, substantial efforts have yet to be made to explain the intellectually wide difference between say Christianity and Hinduism.

ISKCON, for example, has spread its lovely temples far and wide. As a result, the Vaishanav deities, their *pujas*, *aarti* and *prasads* are popularised. The temples are well-constructed, kept clean and are, therefore, welcoming to their devotees whether Hindus or others. But hardly anyone realises and no one explains the invaluable need of the Hindu faith to the world if it wants ongoing peace.

Most people, including the highest to the humblest officials of the United Nations and those that attend its sessions representing their countries have not had any real exposure to

Hinduism. At best, if they visit India, they visit a temple or two and occasionally admire its carvings but are put-off by the oily slippery floors, the avaricious *pandits* and the ill-clad beggars. The importance of the faith cannot be appreciated unless one knows its logic and its reasoning.There are few assumptions in Hindu theology which begins as if it were a science.

As should be well known, the subject of Logic is divided into the Deductive and the Inductive. The former begins with a premise and on its basis its corollaries follow. Say there is one god and he is the only god. Only his followers who do good deeds on earth would be judged on doomsday to be eligible to go to heaven. The followers who did wrong things would have to proceed to hell, but that is their bad luck. If you come across anyone who does not follow the same god but you like the person, you should try to convert him/her to worship the only god without whose judgment he or she cannot possibly reach heaven.

Other than doing deeds as prescribed by the scriptures of your religion, your duty would be to bring into your fold as many non-believers in your god as possible. Additionally, to spread the message of your god, you should get him yet more followers by bringing forth more children in your married life. For the non-believers in your god and religion, there are threats of taking them over. Christianity first clashed with Islam in 711 AD in Spain, conquered the country and onwards the Moors went till they reached Portieres in central France. But for their loyalty to Jesus Christ and the brave generalship of Charles Martel, the Moors would have marched on.

It took centuries for the Spaniards to vacate their land of the Moors. In the meantime, the Christians inspired by their Popes launched the Crusades to recapture their holy land, namely

Jerusalem. There were eight crusades between the years 1095 to 1270 AD. Meanwhile, the Turks from central Asia invaded and conquered parts of Eastern Europe. Turkey was their first and greatest prize besides Albania, Kosovo, Bosnia et al. The history of Europe is a continual saga of war from 711 AD to 1945. The fighting was either Islamic-Christian or intra-Christian.

After World War II ended, the third world war soon began between the USA and the Soviet Union. The weapons used were unique in the annals–escalating nuclear deterrence without firing until the latter side collapsed economically in 1991. In the meanwhile, World War IV had started between the Islamists and the rest of the world. The first shots were fired at the Munich Olympics in 1972 when about a dozen Israeli athletes were killed by terrorists. After visiting all the continents except Latin America, the war appears to be focusing on Europe. At present, it has zeroed in on France.

The conclusive corollary of the deductive premise of the Abrahamic religions is war and more war. On the other hand, Hinduism or the Indic theology is based on inductive logic which begins on the ground and moves up logically towards a conclusion. There is no given premise such as there is only one god. The core of Hinduism or its first version the *Sanatan* (eternal) *dharma* is karma which leads to *bhagya* or fate. Deeds cause destiny is another way of putting it. This equation is remarkably similar to the principle of Physics: for every action, there is an equal and opposite reaction. There was no real question of god originally but there were deities and avatars to enable the worshipper to focus his/her attention. The concept of Bhagwan grew in importance with the advent of the medieval *bhakti* saints. They stressed the concept of *swami* and *das* to enable the common folk to believe in and focus on the object of worship. That helped Hinduism to defend itself first against Islamic conversion attempts and then the efforts of the Christian missionaries.

Every Hindu is free to worship as he likes and where he likes. Virtually every temple functions according to the wishes of its priests; there are innumerable denominations. The lower common denominator–karma, uncannily comes in the way of quick unity. Every Hindu, if he is satisfied with his karmas, is in no hurry to go to the help of another Hindu. As a community, Hindus unite when they feel collectively under threat as they do at present vis-à-vis China.

Fundamentally, the Hindu is not readily inclined to kill any living being, leave alone humans. The reason is the widespread belief in rebirth after rebirth. Even when sacrificing a goat, it could occur to a sensitive individual: what if the animal carries the soul of my late aunt who died three years ago? Hindus are largely vegetarian. The Jains, whom the Hindus do not reject, extend their sympathy even to vegetation especially to items grown under the top soil, say roots.

All in all, an aware Hindu places his faith in self-actualisation for fulfillment in life. This is in contrast to the Abrahamic propensity to collective domination which often leads to conquest through war. Hindu kings or nations have seldom gone out to conquer foreign lands. If they have gone overseas, as the Cholas and the Pandyans of Tamil Nadu did, they spread culture and conducted trade and did not exploit the colony's labour. An example is Indonesia which still displays scenes from the Ramayana, or Cambodia and its Angkor Wat which today is proud to have the finest of Hindu temples.

From Karak to Mathura

THE DISTINGUISHED PHILOSOPHER of history, Sir Arnold Toynbee had said: "In the course of the first Russian occupation of Warsaw, the Russians had built an Eastern Orthodox Christian Cathedral in the city that had been the capital of the once independent Roman Catholic Christian country, Poland. The Russians had done this to give the Poles a continuous ocular demonstration that the Russians were now the masters. After the re-establishment of Poland's independence in 1918, the Poles pulled this cathedral down. I do not blame the Polish government for having pulled down the Russian church. The purpose for which the Russians had built it had not been religious but political, and the purpose had also been intentionally offensive".

The temple in Khyber Pakhtunkhwa that was demolished by miscreants and against which the government of India protested is a mystery. What were the collector, deputy collector and superintendent of police of the Karak District in Pakistan doing while the temple was being demolished and set on fire? Evidently, they were living in the past when the Pakistanis destroyed Hindu temples as a hobby. With difficulty, I was able to collect a short list of the destroyed temples in Pakistan (75 in number) up to the end of the 20th century. After the latest crime had been committed, it appears that Islamabad told the locals to beware as India was now in the mood for Balakots and surgical strikes.

On the other hand, the Islamic feeling is still in line with what Sir Arnold Toynbee has said above. Whichever government is in power, it has the right to decide what to do with an alien or minority place of worship. The latest example is that of Recep Tayyip Erdogan of Turkey, who has recently converted the Hagia Sophia from a museum to a mosque.

Are some Pakistanis living in the medieval age when it was incumbent on a Muslim to destroy anything to do with *butparasti* (idol worship)? Pakistan has demolished 75 temples recorded from 1947 to the year 2000, a figure that does not include Hindu places of worship destroyed or desecrated in what is now Bangladesh. Indian scholars have identified, with the help of chronicled records or epigraphs, the demolition of 3,000 temples in India by invaders which were mostly converted into mosques, using the same base structure. Next to the Qutub Minar in Delhi stands the Quwwatul Islam mosque, which was converted by the first Aibak sultanate after demolishing twenty-seven Jain temples. In the meantime, the law court in Mathura is hearing a petition on the issue of the Krishna Janmabhoomi. The birth place of Krishna is now situated in a small garage-like structure made into a temple. Immediately behind it on a hillock stands the *idgah* built by Aurangzeb in the 17th century. The petition demands that the *idgah* and the hillock underneath be handed over to the Janmasthan Trust. Assuming this issue is resolved, there would still be 2,999 issues unresolved. What should be done about them?

FS Growse, who belonged to the Bengal Civil Service and was Collector of Mathura District in the 1860s, has recorded many things in his exhaustive survey and research about Brajbhoomi. He was so overwhelmed by the vandalism that visited the area repeatedly that he wrote feelingly, although his home was in far-away England. To quote: Thanks to Muhammadan intolerance, there is not a single building of any antiquity either in the city itself or its environs. Its most famous temple, that dedicated to Kesava Deva (Krishna), was destroyed in 1669, the eleventh year of the reign of the iconoclast Aurangzeb (Alamgir). The mosque (*idgah*) erected on its ruins is a building of little architectural value.

Mahmud Ghazni was, however, the first iconoclast to vandalise Mathura. That was in 1017 AD about which Growse wrote:

> If anyone wished to construct a building equal to it, he would not be able to do so without expending a hundred million dinars, and the work would occupy two hundred years, even though the most able and experienced workmen were employed. Orders were given that all the temples should be burnt with naphtha and fire and levelled with the ground. The city was given up to plunder for twenty days. Among the spoils are said to have been five great idols of pure gold with eyes of rubies and adornments of other precious stones, together with a vast number of smaller silver images, which, when broken up, formed a load for more than a hundred camels. The total value of the spoils had been

> estimated at three millions of rupees; while the number of Hindus carried away into captivity exceeded 5,000.

Until the Ayodhya issue was settled by the Supreme Court, no one wanted any mandir-masjid controversy to disturb the litigation. Now that we are past it, the Government of India should consider demanding annulment of the Place of Worship Act 1991, through Parliament. In the meantime, the government could consider appointing a commission of five or seven learned men and women to recommend the fate of the remaining 2,999 temples turned into mosques, which stand as monuments of national humiliation, whether for Hindus, Muslims, Christians, Sikhs or Parsis.

If there are any controversial cases difficult to decide, they could be referred to a committee of archaeologists. Within six months from the beginning, the entire process of recommendations should be completed and returned to the lap of the government of India.

It would be understandable if some Muslims should be reluctant for this. Be that as it may, they should understand that all the disputes between communities were meant to be sorted out by 15 August 1947, with Partition, when the Muslims were given Pakistan and the rest remained in India. For Muslims to now insist on privileges acquired by the fact of their community having been rulers for the best part of 650 years would be grossly unfair. Incidentally, temples turned into mosques were acts of not only plunder, but also blasphemy.

The richly-jewelled idols taken from the pagan temples were transferred to Agra and there placed beneath the steps leading to the Nawab Begum Sahib's mosque, in order that they might ever be pressed underfoot by the true believers.

Most of the idols were from the just-destroyed Kesava Deva temple, built at the spot where the popular *avatar* was believed to have been born some 3,400 years ago. If Mahmud Ghazni was a *jaahil* or a barbarian, one might have been inclined to overlook his outrage and excuse him. But both Al Barooni and Utbi, who were chroniclers and lived in Ghazni's times, certified that Mahmud was devout and built beautiful mosques in his Ghazni.

Jinnah called the Aligarh Muslim University "the arsenal of Muslim India"

PRIME MINISTER MODI addressing the students of Aligarh Muslim University on its centenary was a compliment to the controversial institution. Its academic and educational achievements are well-known but those alone cannot speak of its health. Some of the Aligarh alumni, when in Delhi, call on me from time to time which helps me to get a feel of the goings-on at the University.

A doctor assesses the current health of a patient not by his achievements but by the latest symptoms. The protests held by the Aligarh students against the CAA some months ago might have been legitimate but, for up to 70 persons to be injured in a temple of learning was tragic. The CAA (Citizenship Amendment Act) was seen as a communal law because Muslims were not included for immediate citizenship if they arrived, whether from Pakistan, Bangladesh or anywhere else.

How could they be? They had demanded and voted for Partition in 1945-46. The students from Aligarh had gone as far as Punjab to campaign for the Muslim League whose one point manifesto was Pakistan. Some Punjabis enquired from some of the students as to what was there for them as young campaigners for the Partition. They were from UP and their province would not be included in the new homeland. The students' reported reply was: "Why, we will all gain by creating a New Medina. The world does not have a *khalifa* at present".

No wonder Qaid-e-Azam Jinnah called Aligarh University the "arsenal of Muslim India", a generous *shabashi*. At the same time, the students expected Muslims to be included in the CAA. Now, a common person might not realise it but surely educated university students should. And certainly, their professors should have explained to them.

Perhaps, the teachers as well as the students can be excused on grounds of being deeply imbued in the history of their university, and of course the thinking of the founder of the institution. Sir Syed Ahmad Khan was no doubt a learned man and an earnest well-wisher of his people. In 1887 at Meerut, and at Lucknow in 1888, the distinguished leader declared that the Hindus and Muslims were separate nations. The Congress was essentially a Hindu political party and Muslims should avoid joining it. On an earlier occasion, Sir Syed had said that since the British took political power from the Muslim sultans and nawabs, when they withdrew from India, the current rulers should return the rule over the country to Muslims.

The late leader Syed Shahabuddin had clearly written in a letter to the editor of a national daily that if it comes to a choice between identity and development, Muslims would prefer their identity. No doubt, this view was expressed by one leader only. However, faith was placed by virtually all the religious clergy for over a thousand years in *taqlid* (orthodoxy) and it had simultaneously prohibited *ijtihad* (reinterpretation). The prime minister should not be disappointed if his strong message for development is not paid sufficient heed to by the Aligarh students.

The Aligarh Movement was launched by Syed Ahmad Khan in the 1860s. In terms of its significance and consequences for India, this was the most important of all movements launched by the Muslims in modern history. The movement has been called the "Aligarh Movement" because its headquarters were at Aligarh. Prof MS Jain in his research monograph *The Aligarh Movement* (1965) asks: "Why did we not develop into a homogeneous nation and why did the Muslims of India, generally speaking, chalk out a path different from that of the other communities in India? The movement of Muslim regeneration initiated by Sir Syed Ahmad Khan provides the answer".

The renowned historian, Prof AL Srivastava, in his preface to the above document expresses similar sentiments in the words: "Aligarh's role has consequently been one of unabashed reaction and communal partisanship during India's struggle for freedom against British imperialism and also to a lesser extent, after the attainment of Independence in August 1947".

In the words of the historian KM Panikkar: "The Aligarh movement, which is the central factor of Islamic renaissance in India, had two very important results. It was the first step towards the integration of Indian Islam. The dispersed Muslim population in different parts of India had now a central institution which provided them with a common intellectual background, and fostered a common ideology. It was the Aligarh man who was the spearhead of Muslim movement in every corner of

India. In the second step, Aligarh elevated Urdu to the position of a national language for Indian Islam. Thus provided with a separate language and a special ideology, the Muslims were able, in due course, to claim to be a separate nation".

Upon his retirement from government service in 1876, Sir Syed Ahmad Khan was knighted and made a member of the Governor General's Legislative Council (1878-1883). In this capacity he successfully drove his viewpoint that Muslims should receive separate nominations to the local self-governments created by Lord Ripon. The Indian National Congress was founded towards the end of Syed's life. Commenting on its agenda in his speeches made at Lucknow and Meerut in 1887-88, Ahmad Khan said: "The proposals of the Congress are exceedingly inexpedient for a country which is inhabited by two different nations, the Hindus and the Muslims. Now suppose all the English were to leave India...it is necessary that one of them should conquer the other and thrust it down. To hope that both could remain equal is to desire the impossible and the inconceivable".

Richard Symonds who came out with his book *The Making of Pakistan*, (Faber & Faber, London, 1949) on the morrow of the emergence of Pakistan has written: "In politics he (Syed Ahmad Khan) had stated that Muslims were a nation who could not and must not be submerged in a system of government by majority vote. The Pakistanis rightly claim him as one of the fathers of their country".

In the *Aligarh Institute Gazette* of 22 Sept 1893, Sir Syed wrote: "Mahomedans may accept English supremacy because they have been conquered by Englishmen, but who is to make them submit to the supremacy of the Hindus, whom for 700 years they regarded their slaves". Sir Syed laid down as a matter of policy for the Muslims: undiluted loyalty to the British regime; no truck with the Indian National Congress and pursuit of modern education. This was followed by Muslims until 1906.

In conformity with this view, Syed Ahmad Khan felt that India occupied an intermediate position between *Dar al-Islam* and *Dar al-Harb.* According to Qureshi, member of National Assembly of Pakistan, Syed Ahmad Khan laid the foundation of the interpretation of Islam to suit the modern mind. This theme was later on developed by Syed Ameer Ali (a scholar of Islam), and poet Iqbal. Qureshi continues: "Aligarh gave the Muslim country a new hope, a new sense of mission. From the deepest despair it pulled the Muslim out into a new field of fruitful activity". Indeed Aligarh was the cradle of the feeling of nationalism among the Muslims because it kept alive the idea of a well-integrated Muslim community in the subcontinent. Prof Wilfred Smith, a scholar of Islam says that by 1941 Aligarh had become the emotional centre of Pakistan; whereas Sir Aga Khan, one of the founders of the All-India Muslim League, claims that the independent, sovereign nation of Pakistan was born in the Muslim University of Aligarh.

After the introduction of the Nagri script in Uttar Pradesh in 1900, a demand developed for the formation of a Muslim political association. Ghulam-us-Saqlain, a graduate of Aligarh and a Pakistani Urdu writer, wrote the following in his journal *Asr-i-Jadid* (Modern Voice): "Intelligent Musalmans will readily admit the necessity for the establishment of a Muhammadan Political Association. Owing to the want of such an association, the interests of the Muhammadan community have already suffered in a variety of ways and are still being trampled underfoot; some of the instances being the Hindi-Urdu controversy and exclusion of Persian from the Allahabad University and the paucity of Musalman members in the Municipal and Local Boards".

Once a Waqf, Always a Waqf

FORMER UNION MINISTER for Minority Affairs Mukhtar Abbas Naqvi sometime ago had announced that the government would be setting up Waqf Boards for Jammu, Kashmir and Ladakh. Naqvi had also stated that all these decades, the dynastic rule of the Abdullahs and later the Mufti family had exercised control over Muslim affairs and prevented them from being administered under the *waqf* arrangement. The government's move according to Naqvi was an attempt to bring them under the umbrella of the *waqf*.

It is, therefore, instructive to understand what a *waqf* really is and the nature of this institution, which is spread across the country owning between five to six acres of urban land. Literally, the word *waqf* means standing, stopping or halting. *The Dictionary of Islam* by Thomas Patrick Hughes (Rupa & Company, Delhi; 1999) explains the term *waqf*. It is the appropriation or dedication of property for charitable uses and service of God; an endowment. The object of such an endowment or appropriation must be of a perpetual nature, and no property or land can be sold or transferred. Just as when a person builds a mosque, his right of property is extinguished as soon as prayers have been recited in the building so, too, is the case when an asset is donated to a *waqf*.

The root of this institution lies in Prophet Muhammad's exhortation in his lifetime for contributions for waging jihad. He had demanded such donations from his followers in Medina. Professor Asaf AA Fyzee, in his book *Outlines of Muhammadan Law* (OUP, Delhi; 1999), quotes the traditional source of *Bukhari*, a great scholar of Hadith, according to whom the earliest *waqf* was that of Umar, the Second Caliph. This *waqf* became the basis of the law on the subject. To quote:

Ibn Omar reported, "Omar ibn al-Khattab got land in Khaybar; so he came to the Prophet, peace and blessings of Allah be on him, to consult him about it. He said, 'O Messenger of Allah! I have got land in Khaybar than which I have never obtained more valuable property; what dost thou advise about it?' He said, 'If thou likest, make the property itself to remain inalienable, and give (the profit from) it in charity'."

While charity might have been the original intention of *waqf*, the institution gradually became an instrument of securing a source of revenue for protecting and promoting Islam. *The Oxford History of Islam* (OUP, New York, 1999), characterises *waqf* as an Islamic source of revenue. To quote:

> A study of north-central Anatolia in the 15th and 16th centuries provides a deeper understanding of the workings of the land and tax systems. When the Ottomans obtained control of these regions in the mid 15th century, they had to concede to the Turkish military rulers and Muslim religious leaders ownership

> rights to the land. In the course of the next century and a half, the state struggled to dispossess the local notables and to reassign the tax rights to *timar* (Ottoman Land grants) holders appointed by the central government. Still, much property remained *mulk* (private property) or *waqfs* (endowments), but these tended to be fragmented small holdings often in the possession of the central government. The Ottomans thus gained control over the *ulema* and made them functionaries of the state, and they also co-opted the leading Sufi brotherhoods.

The representatives of spiritual other-worldly power thus became the protectors of the state. In comparison with other Muslim societies this was an extraordinary organisational achievement, but came at a high price. Insofar as the *ulema* and leading Sufis became functionaries of the state, they ceased to represent the Muslim masses and could no longer protect them from abuses of political power. They were now servants of the state and defenders of Ottoman legitimacy and could not effectively resist corruption in the government. Becoming a class of functionaries dependent on government patronage for their offspring and students, they became a powerful interest group within the state itself.

In due course, *waqf* developed into an instrument of aggression. Professor Joseph Schacht of Columbia University, New York, in his *Introduction to Islamic Law*; (Universal Law Publishing Co., Indian reprint, 1997) has the following to write:

> The *waqf* is a good example of the composite nature of the raw material of Islamic law and of the qualitatively new character which its institutions acquired; the *waqf* has one of its roots in contributions to the holy war which Muhammad had incessantly demanded from his followers in Medina.

1920 onwards, the impetus of modernist jurisprudence and modernist legislative movement inspired by it came from Egypt. The most important milestones of this legislation in Egypt were Acts No 25 of 1920 and No 25 of 1929 on the law of family. Act No 462 of 1955 abolished the *kadis'* tribunals (together with all denominational jurisdictions of personal status). This bill aimed at restricting polygamy and the husband's right to unilaterally repudiate his wife. This reshaping of Islamic law by modernist legislation evoked and inspired similar movements in other countries of the Middle East like Sudan, Jordan, Lebanon, Syria, Iraq and Libya. The laws enacted in those countries occasionally went further than their Egyptian prototypes.

The application of English legal reasoning to institutions of Islamic law led to difficulties, as in the case of *waqf*. An essential feature of the Hanafi *waqf* is the permanence of its purpose, especially if the beneficiaries are, for instance, the descendants of the founder, the poor or some other subsidiary beneficiaries. The Privy Council, however, held in 1894 that the ultimate reversion to the poor was illusory, and that this kind of 'family *waqf*' had to be treated as 'simple gift' of inalienable life-interests to remote unborn generations of descendants which was forbidden in Islamic law and was, therefore, invalid. This decision invalidated a fundamental institution of Islamic law of great practical importance and created much dismay in India. The legislature had to pass the Mussalman *Waqf* Validating Act of 1913, restoring the doctrine of Islamic jurisprudence concerning the family *waqf*.

French colonies were even more dynamic and drastic especially after getting their independence. Tunisia under

President Habib Bourguiba abolished *waqfs* in 1956. Professor Asaf AA Fyzee, in his book *Outlines of Muhammadan Law,* commenting at length on the developments in *waqf* across several countries, said:

> The importance of the institution will be better understood if we take into consideration the enormous extent of waqf land or the possessions of the Dead Hand in the various countries of Islam. In the Turkey of 1925, three-fourths of the arable land, estimated at 50,000,000 Turkish pounds, was endowed as waqf. At the end of the 19th century, one-half of the cultivable land in Algiers was dedicated. Similarly, in Tunisia one-third and in Egypt one-eighth of the cultivated soil was 'in the ownership of God'. But it was already realised by the beginning of the 20th century, first by France and later in Turkey and Egypt, that the possession of the Dead Hand spelled ruin. The institution of waqf was in some respects a handicap to the natural growth and development of a healthy national economy.

In 1830, the French government took over the harbours in Algiers, and later in Morocco. Elsewhere, government control was made more stringent. In 1924, the Turkish republic abolished the Ministry of *Waqfs* and it was taken over by a general directory, or by the secular state administration. Muhammad Ali in Egypt first confiscated all agricultural *waqfs,* and in 1924, the *Waqf* Ministry came directly under the control of parliament. In Russia, *waqfs* existed in Muslim districts for centuries, but after the revolution were confiscated and declared state property.

Fyzee took the opportunity to give his views on the nature of *waqf* as well as its effects on the people and society:

> We must consider briefly the advantages and disadvantages of the institution. The religious motive of *waqf* is the origin of the legal fiction that *waqf* property belongs to Almighty God; the economic ruin that it brings about is indicated by the significant phrase 'The Dead Hand'. *Waqf* to some extent ameliorates poverty, but it has also its dark side. When a father provides a certain income for his children and descendents, the impulse to seek education and the initiative to improve their lot gradually decrease. Charitable aid often keeps people away from industry, and lethargy breeds degeneration. Furthermore, some people who desire fame by making foundations and endowments obtain property by shady means, amounting even to extortion and exploitation. Agricultural land deteriorates in the course of time; no one is concerned with keeping it in good trim; the yield lessens, and even perpetual leases come to be recognised. In India, instances of the mismanagement of *waqfs*, of the worthlessness of *mutawallis* (managers), and of the destruction of *waqf* property have often come before the courts. Considering all these matters, it can by no means be said that the institution of *waqf* as a whole has been an unmixed blessing to the community.

Everything stated earlier points to the need for summary abolition of *waqfs* in India. It was a colonial instrument of raising revenue for the *ulema* in order that oligarchic regimes could keep their grip over power. *Waqfs* have been abolished in one country after another, including Muslim countries. In India, the institution has been abused for attracting and sustaining a feudal class in a conquered land. With the advent of Partition and the creation of a holy land for Indian Muslims, the *waqf* became an eyesore of discrimination between one minority and the rest of the Indian people. When soon after independence, the princely states were integrated into the national mainstream and the *zamindaris* and the *jagirdaris* were abolished, where is the justification for perpetuating this parasitic institution?

Anti-Semitism–a form of Racism

FOR SOMEONE WHO had Jewish friends in college and who was given a roaring start to his career by a Jewish firm called BN Elias & Co, it is very difficult to comprehend anti-Semitism. The few Jewish Americans I have met were perfectly cordial. I have enjoyed my holiday in the Jewish land, especially Jerusalem. At Calvary Hill, I realised that Jesus Christ was born a Jew, lived as a Jew, was betrayed by a Jew and was crucified while a Jew. There were no Christians when all this happened. Christianity received a boost when the Roman Emperor Constantine became a Christian in around the year 325 AD. He shifted to what is now called Istanbul; when the Emperor founded the city, it was called Constantinople. The change came when the Seljuks conquered the region. Subsequently, about the middle of the 15th century—1453 AD precisely—when the Turks overran Constantinople, the city's name was changed to what it is now. Yet the headquarters of the Eastern Church are still at Istanbul as those of the Roman Catholic Church are at the Vatican. St Peter and St Paul, two outstanding apostles of Jesus Christ and many others were Jews to start with. Why this anti-Semitism then?

It is true that the Jews do not accept Jesus as the son of God. They cannot, as they place their faith in Jehovah as their only god. They also do not recognise Christ as the Messiah whose final arrival the Jews still await. In the past, they had obligations to the Roman emperors who expected all citizens under their imperial umbrella to look upon them (i.e., the Roman rulers) as gods on earth. Regardless of reasons, why has this prejudice carried on and on, century after century?

The Jews had undergone untold oppression at the hands of the Egyptians and their Pharaohs for centuries until they were rescued by Prophet Moses. Yet, centuries after that episode, many Jews happily settled in Egypt, especially Alexandria. We Indians were suppressed and often also oppressed for the best part of seven centuries by invaders; our country was partitioned, but we do not hate anyone. Historian Sonja Weinberg says that Jews have, over the centuries, conspired to 'Judaize' the world. However, it is difficult to comprehend this. They did not have their own exclusive country or an army, nor does Judaism believe in converting people of other faiths to its own–unlike Christianity and Islam.

Anti-Semitism has clearly racialist overtones unlike anti-Judaism, which is purely religious or having to do with matters of faith. Then why do Christians or Muslims feel delighted if some Jews convert to their respective religions? Do the converted undergo a racial metamorphosis? Some scholars of different races have felt that Jews are of an inferior race. If that were so, how have so many Jews won many a Nobel

Prize, which is awarded by a Christian foundation? Jews have been alleged to be leeches of money, guilty of usury and greedy bankers; Nazi Germany's propaganda minister Josef Goebbels repeatedly called them parasites.

But why limit blame for anti-Semitism to the Nazis alone? Martin Luther, who initiated the Christian Reformation in the mid-16th century, recommended in writing a pogrom against the Jews. He went on to write: "We are at fault in not slaying them". Historian Paul Johnson described Luther's diatribe as "a giant step forward on the road to the Holocaust" by Nazi Germany.

Anti-Semitism wasn't exclusive to Germany. The last Russian Czar Nicholas-II once declared that "One-third of the (Russian) Jews must die, one-third must emigrate and one-third be converted to Christianity". What could be the logic of such hatred? Karl Marx, himself the grandson of a Jewish rabbi, in his essay "On the Jewish Question" equated Judaism with capitalism. Father Coughlin, an American priest, described President Franklin Roosevelt's New Deal of the 1930s to revive the US economy after the 1929 Great Depression as, "a Jewish financial conspiracy". Evidently, there has been something unusual about the Jews which aroused resentment among many different quarters, plus those with substantial Jewish blood including tall intellectuals like Karl Marx. What can it be?

The German philosopher Friedrich Nietzsche put his finger on a near-possibility as to cause of anti-Semitism or anti-Judaism. Here is what he wrote: "The whole problem of the Jews exists only in nation states, for here their energy and higher intelligence, their accumulated capital of spirit and will, gathered from generation to generation through a long schooling in suffering, must become so preponderant as to arouse mass envy and hatred. In almost all contemporary nations therefore—in direct proportion to the degree to which they act up nationalistically—the literal obscenity of leading the Jews to slaughter as scapegoats of every conceivable public and internal misfortune is spreading".

In short, the Jews are a transnational people and have been more committed to their faith than to any country they have resided in except, of course, Israel. The Muslims are more openly supra-national, with their *ummah* being all important. So also are the Communists, with their slogan "Workers of the world unite".

There are other explanations for anti-Semitism, which has not died despite all claims of modernity and progress. Religious philosophers over the centuries have stated other reasons. One view is that anti-Semitism serves to remind Jews that they are eternally distinct from other nations and that God is ultimately the only one upon whom Jews can rely.

More uncompromising historian-philosophers say that humanity had many gods in ancient times, allowing for a diversity of human belief and ethics, termed "a kind of sacred relativism" by some intellectuals. The advent of Judaism is held as the beginning of monotheism, and the imposition of a God who is all demanding, judgmental, and intolerant of any other way of worship or living. Ardent Jews regard this as their singularly greatest contribution to humanity. George Steiner, a literary critic and professor of comparative literature at Oxford and Cambridge, argues that this came with a price—hatred of Jews and Judaism.

Dividing Pakistan: An Advantage?

IT IS ONE thing to admire Bangabandhu Mujibur Rahman; to applaud the secession of East Pakistan is another, especially so from the viewpoint of India. The late Prime Minister Morarji Desai had complained that we had inherited one Pakistan but Indira has given us two. He evidently did not approve of the popular delight in dividing Pakistan and having two Islamic countries neighbouring India instead of one.

The pros and cons of this issue have not been studied sufficiently. First, Bangladesh's secession need not have been inevitable had Islamabad made greater use of brains rather than bullets. One may recall the amalgamation of Punjab, Sindh, NWFP and Balochistan into a single province to create a balance against the populous East Pakistan. Instead, had the East been reorganised into say four provinces for effective governance, there would have been four capitals, four chief ministers and so on. Whether Sheikh Mujibur Rahman could then have risen as an unquestioned *rehnuma-e-azam* (great leader) of the East is doubtful. If the East was allowed to retain the foreign exchange it earned through jute and its products plus any other exports, a major genuine grouse would have disappeared. It would have gladly paid for its imports then. Also, Urdu and Bengali could have both been made official languages.

Pakistan's generals, whether Field Marshal Ayub Khan or Yahya Khan could not see through Zulfikar Ali Bhutto's game of wanting to get rid of East Pakistan so that he could be the prime minister. Even as late as 1971, President Yahya Khan could have negotiated with the Bangabandhu for an amicable settlement. Instead, they sent General Tikka Khan to Dhaka to perpetrate one of the biggest pogroms in the annals of history. At the end of it their Foreign Minister Bhutto gave an extraordinarily theatrical performance at the United Nations about fighting India for a thousand years, his eyes flooded with tears, to ward off any allegation that he had instigated the pogrom for secession.

Before the 1971 pogrom not many people infiltrated into Assam and Bengal across our eastern borders. This weaponless invasion began when the poor in Bangladesh awoke to the fact that they were on their own. They had no hope of even going to West Pakistan. Hence, they began migrating to wherever they could. Some political leaders in Kolkata actively helped them to obtain ration cards and other documents in exchange of votes. To all this was added the fear spread by environmentalists that in a few decades, 17 percent of Bangladesh's land area would be submerged by the sea.

A wife of a tea garden manager in the Sylhet district of the East had written an interesting book on the plantation life, including how she and her husband and their two children escaped when fighting began in 1971. Raihana A Hasan while not expressing any hatred, showed contempt for the locals repeatedly describing them as short and dark. Nearly all the managers of the gardens were from the western wing. Only the few estates owned by locals had Bengali managers. All in all, East Pakistan was a millstone around Pakistan's neck, mostly because of prejudice. In the strategic sense, an undivided Pakistan was advantageous to India.

Our military intervention was no doubt humanitarian. For Bengalis of any faith, understandably, it was also emotional; while for many Indians it was a matter of joy of breaking up an antagonistic neighbour. As events have unfolded recently, proponents of the intervention would argue: what about Chinese influence? Would it not have come to our eastern border as it has on our west, had Bangladesh not been separated from Pakistan? Here, one must point to the fact that Bangladesh has rustled up armed forces far in excess of its actual needs for the possibility of its collusion with the Chinese—should a war with that country happen in the future which cannot be ruled out. In the immediate aftermath of the 1971 victory, the sheer euphoria and triumphal feeling at having sundered the hated enemy was overpowering. "*Saakshat Durga hai*" was how Atal Bihari Vajpayee, who would go on to be the nation's prime minister, described Indira Gandhi immediately after India's lightning decimation of Pakistan in the 1971 war.

India's intervention has landed itself with a serious strategic problem. With the erstwhile East Pakistan as its eastern wing, Pakistan was always unbalanced. With its severance, Pakistan became a more cohesive entity. It would have wasted itself trying to preserve its eastern territory, but after 1971, began carrying its jihad into India in keeping with its doctrine of "bleeding India by a thousand cuts". This fact is not appreciated by the peaceniks and those naive enough to believe that "people to people contact" and mouthing of empty platitudes will solve all problems between India and Pakistan.

Pakistan's ISI also operates with impunity in Bangladesh, carrying out anti-India activities in collusion with the Islamist terror groups based there. Then there is the ever-present menace of infiltration, which has the twin objectives of grabbing living space for Bangladesh's population and altering the demography of our North-Eastern states, which face the alarming prospect of being swamped by Bangladeshis. One should not be surprised if some day Bangladesh claims India's North-East to be an 'integral part' of Bangladesh. Sheikh Mujibur had years earlier written that the economy of East Bengal would not be fully viable without Assam being a part of it.

The Hindus in Bangladesh are not treated well. India, the country whose sacrifices made the birth of Bangladesh possible is looked upon with suspicion. Why have things come to this pass? This is so because the political handling of the aftermath of 1971 war was naïve, to say the least. Indira Gandhi left her policy-making to the *Panch Pyare*, i.e., her five advisors, who botched a historic opportunity to settle Pakistan. In Bangladesh, we put all our eggs earlier in Sheikh Mujibur Rahman's basket. With his assassination, we lost all our bargaining power. Fortunately, Mujib's daughter, Sheikh Hasina, is not anti-India as Begum Khaleda Zia was and continues to be.

Unfortunately, foreign policy in India has hitherto been an exclusive preserve of the Nehru dynasty, with often disastrous results. It is only after 2014 that we are seeing a marked change in this regard with commensurate change in India's stature in the world. Foreign policy calls for greater transparency and greater debate, both within Parliament and also outside in the media and amongst the think tanks.

While thinking about foreign policy in the context of Bangladesh, I am sure as to what might follow after the current Prime Minister of Bangladesh quits office. Sheikh Hasina remembers her father, how her country was liberated, and the importance of pursuing a moderate foreign policy, especially towards India. The reason for sounding this note of caution is that an Islamic country has few policy options. They have to work within the framework of what the Quran says. True democracy is not possible, nor is genuine socialism. When Islam was born, there were only kings and sheikhs. Times have changed since, but the scriptures have not. Therefore, when rulers run out of options, they take refuge in militarism or Islamic extremism, as did President Zia-ul-Haq of Pakistan.

Beware of Pakistan's Softening

NORMALLY, ANYTHING THAT leads to peace should be welcome. So, we should welcome the fact that Pakistan has agreed to cessation of ongoing hostilities with us and honour the ceasefire pact of 2003.

Yet, one must interject a note of caution here. This is because quite a few Indians, including expert observers, have interpreted the venom from Islamabad on Kashmir for years as revenge for India dismembering their country in 1971. In actual fact, as soon as the anger of defeat was forgotten, the Pakistanis were relieved that the dark, short people—as the Bengalis are contemptuously referred to by Pakistanis—who were a majority of their population, were finally got rid of.

Poet Muhammad Iqbal, who was also a leading light of the Muslim League as its president, had in 1930 at Prayagraj (then Allahabad) proposed a separate Muslim homeland which comprised only the north-western provinces. He made no mention of Bengal or any part thereof. The larger Pakistan was for Jinnah's glorification; he began by dreaming of six provinces—four in the west and two in the east, including Assam. Through his League colleague Syed Muhammad Saadulla who was the Premier of Assam for several years after 1939, he had nearly succeeded in recording that the *adivasis* were not Hindus but animists. This was to bring down the Hindu percentage of population and draw Assam into Pakistan when the moment of decision came. When Jinnah could not get Assam, except the district of Sylhet, Bengal and Punjab were divided by Sir Cyril Radcliffe, the lawyer dispatched by London. Jinnah was sorely disappointed at getting what he called "a moth-eaten Pakistan".

Here, it has to be iterated that Jinnah did not represent the ultimate choice of any Pakistani except the Gujarati-speaking businessmen like the Khojas and Memons, who wanted to get rich quickly by avoiding business competition against Indian business communities by going over to the new state, where they would have to compete only against the Punjabi and Sindhi farmers. For the rest, Jinnah pleaded brilliantly for those Muslims who wanted or half-wished a separate homeland. This was Jinnah's role in actuality; his fees being his place in history's hall of fame. Fortunately for him, he died within 13 months of Independence. The word *muhajir*, a term for Muslims from UP and Bihar migrating to Pakistan, came into circulation soon thereafter. But *muhajirs* soon found themselves not only unwelcome but also the target of ethnic hostility in the newly-carved out Muslim homeland. Jinnah's deputy Liaquat Ali Khan from UP, was assassinated a mere four years after Pakistan had been carved out.

What prevails in Pakistan now is the will of the Punjabis

who are two-thirds of the country's population. Their need for Kashmir has kept the country together and papered over their differences. They portray India as a great threat to the survival of Pakistan and thus justify the indispensability of the army as the country's guardian.

If one looks at the latest ceasefire agreement, one would conclude that for Islamabad it is a temporary move to hopefully tide over the crises the country is facing. The moment Pakistan's rulers are able to find some way of relief for these crises, the current agreement will turn into a mere piece of paper. One reason for Pakistan's softening could be that its rulers realise that China has overplayed its hand, whether with India, Taiwan or South China Sea and that the USA has reacted strongly, though so far only in words. Otherwise, there is no explanation for Beijing to kick off a confrontation in Ladakh during the winter. It could have waited until after the spring to exercise its options which were three: to try and grab some strategically useful land points, to ease off by extracting some other concessions or by continuing to harass the Indian forces by creating local points that would pose a threat. Similarly, Islamabad wants to cool off vis-à-vis New Delhi until China warms up again after arriving at some settlement with the USA. If not, the rulers would wait for circumstances to change; for a true *momin*, his faith in Allah the Merciful is infinite. We must not compare it with the mind of a thinking or reticent Hindu.

Another possibility might be that Pakistan's real ruler, General Bajwa, wants to ease India's pressure on his eastern front and use it to settle his scores with Baluchistan, rather like General Tikka had tried to do in East Pakistan in 1971. Bajwa may have been advised that the Baloch province is so rich in resources that it could greatly help in solving Pakistan's economic problems. But to exploit these resources, it would take time, peace and complete control. Unless Islamabad takes some drastic steps, how can it keep the economic wheels of Pakistan rolling? If it depends on Chinese loans, Pakistan could become a Beijing protectorate, inch by inch, as one has already begun to see with the China-Pakistan Economic Corridor (CPEC) coming into play.

Pakistan on the Boil

THERE IS AN unreported civil war raging in Pakistan. The country is on the boil as never before, except when its eastern wing rebelled and seceded in 1971. Several weeks ago there were huge processions in the cities of Sindh with a few Indian flags also being waved. Recently, violent crowds were on the rampage in Karachi, Rawalpindi and Islamabad. This agitation has already killed a hundred odd people, including four policemen; many others were injured and some abducted. Prime Minister Imran Khan's regime has blocked social media access across the country, reflecting the state of affairs. These protests are ostensibly because of the French government's stand that the *Charlie Hebdo* cartoons of Prophet Muhammad, published in 2013, are an inalienable part of the freedom of press.

Anti-government rioting in Pakistan is being orchestrated by the Tehreek-e-Labbaik Pakistan. One of the newer Pakistani extremist outfits, also called the TLP, is a Barelvi party founded in 2015 by a virulent cleric Khadim Rizvi. It is an extremist Sunni organisation advocating hatred of all others, including Shias. Khadim Rizvi passed away in November 2020, but his 26-year-old son Saad Rizvi now leads the agitation. The TLP also contested elections; it got 22 lakh votes in the 2018 polls.

The rioting has made most French citizens leave Pakistan. Whether Islamabad's misrule is approaching its climax or not is not India's business. What is our business, though, is the apprehension of desperate common folk crossing over from Sindh to Rajasthan. We are familiar with infiltration from Pakistan's former eastern wing and have not been able to do much about those millions illegally settled in India. Do we wish to risk another episode, this time from the western wing? The area beyond Jaisalmer in Rajasthan is not fenced while other portions have barbed wire fencing.

What should worry Pakistan is that within only five years of being formed, the TLP has gained immense ground and now confronts the Pakistani state head on. Some observers say this is leading to a situation worse than in even neighbouring Afghanistan. Pakistan's internal order is far from stable. Prime Minister Imran Khan is clearly reluctant to act against the TLP, symptomatic of faultlines in a nuclear weapon state. It appears that TLP is either powerfully backed or is actually popular.

Regardless of the current agitation, Pakistan's economy has been steadily eroding. Take a micro aspect: President Ayub Khan in the 1960s had apprehended that the country would run out of beef unless consumption was restrained. Ayub followed up on this by declaring Fridays as meatless days. Over time, American aid to Pakistan rose to four billion dollars. This US largesse might have helped import essentials other than military purchases. Life in Pakistan went along merrily, but eventually this aid declined and ended, forcing it to turn to China. The Chinese alternative is proving exorbitant in terms of interest payments as well as likely dilution of sovereignty. Pakistanis have never had the habit of paying taxes. Any revenue from those who paid was welcomed by the state.

The Pakistan army is exorbitantly expensive due to its commercial ventures. Senior officers are not only soldiers but also run profitable enterprises. Since the advent to power of General Zia-ul-Haq, many institutions in Pakistan, particularly the military, underwent radicalisation. The armed forces, like their Indian counterparts, inherited a fine tradition from the British but have now become part-soldiers and part-Islamists. Such an army cannot be relied upon by the state in situations like the current one. Many countries mix religion and government, but mixing religion with the armed forces is fraught with disaster.

None of this should come as a surprise. Qaid-e-Azam Jinnah was an excellent advocate and a political debater, but knew no governance. In any case, he was dying of tuberculosis when Pakistan came into being. His successor Liaquat Ali Khan was a zamindar, not a nation-builder and was assassinated before long. It was political musical chairs thereafter, with no prime minister lasting long. General Ayub Khan seized power, a decisive proof of governance failure.

Ayub was replaced by General Yayha Khan who presided over the secession of East Pakistan, now Bangladesh. Zulfikar Ali Bhutto as PM played for himself and not for Pakistan. He tricked and murdered his way to electoral victory. Zia-ul-Haq overthrew and hanged him to become President for ten years.

Zia Islamised Pakistan, but beyond that did nothing for nation-building. Pakistan has had three Constitutions, all of which begin by stating that the country's sovereignty belongs to Allah the Merciful, something even Saudi Arabia's Constitution does not do.

Pakistan has had three long phases of direct military rule. General Musharraf, on the morrow of the September 11, 2001, terror attacks in New York, switched from Islam to America. He had no choice. By then Pakistan was already a mess and nothing could be done to reform or reorganise it. Pakistan by its very nature is an artificial state, created by a brilliant lawyer who knew nothing of history, politics and governance. All he was obsessed with was his place in the hall of history.

Changing Parties

APPREHENSIONS HAVE BEEN expressed that the BJP's ideology will get mixed up, if not actually vitiated by the entry of politicians brought up in an alien thought process. The chances of such confusion are few for the simple reason that most of the new members joining the BJP happen to be Hindu. There would, therefore, be no contradiction between their own private lives and what should be in their public life and political expression. In contrast, if a person like me were to join say the Revolutionary Socialist Party (RSP) at the age of fifty, for a year or two, I would not know whether I was coming or going; it would be somewhat traumatic.

I have been brought up in the belief of karma, and in the RSP I would have to switch to faith in a "permanent revolution" as preached by Leon Trotsky, Vladimir Lenin's favourite number two until he lived. This favourite leader wanted to go on with the revolution until he had converted the whole world to communism. If one reads the *Das Kapital*, the Bible of Marxism, one would come across the foundational tenet: "From each according to his ability to each according to his need". The words are simple, but the message behind could take an average politician some exercise in mental digestion.

A similar challenge had faced Dr BR Ambedkar who had resolved that he would not like to die a Hindu. In that case, the question arose—which religion should he and his many followers convert to? Babasaheb adopted the thinking method of *reductio ad absurdum* (proving the falsity of a premise by showing that its logical consequence is absurd or contradictory). He took up Christianity first and rejected it because it was of a foreign origin; it would, therefore, have a denationalising effect on his followers. Moreover, by having more Christians, Dr Ambedkar felt that they would add to supporters of the British rulers. Islam also had a foreign origin; more Muslims also could mean greater support for the creation of Pakistan. With this reasoning, his eventual choice fell on Buddhism.

For politicians, joining the BJP is like coming home; politically what they should have believed in and now they are doing so. If they are committed to secularism, they can continue to be so. The question of Church and State being separate or otherwise does not arise in the case of the temple. Virtually every temple can follow its own ritual of worship so how can it influence the government? In any case, Hinduism has never had a habit or tradition of dabbling in politics. State governance was the exclusive function of the ruler. But the fact is that since the early sun rose in the mists of time, the Indic ethos has been Hindu or what one calls Sanatan or Vedic. That came through in the reasoning of Dr Ambedkar discussed above.

Traditionally, in the West, especially in America, the common folk identified Indians as Hindus and then enquired whether one was a Hindu Muslim, a Hindu Christian or a Hindu Hindu. Some Nehruvians might have been embarrassed, but most of the time the identity of India has been Hindu. The birth of Pakistan intensified this trend.

The Hindu Mahasabha was founded in 1915 after the Muslim League was given birth by Lord Curzon in Dacca in 1906 (now Dhaka) after inducing the Nawab Salimullah of Dacca with a loan of £ 100,000. The Bharatiya Jana Sangh came into being under the leadership of Dr Syama Prasad Mookerjee in 1951. The RSS helped him with some whole-time workers. In 1977, to fight the general election immediately after the end of the Emergency, the Jana Sangh, like several other parties, merged with a new combine called the Janata Party. In 1980, the Jana Sanghis left this party to form the Bharatiya Janata Party. To begin with, its manifesto was based around Gandhian Socialism.

The centre point of the party's ideology is the nation above all else. It is the anti-thesis of the supra-nationalist communism. The Islamic supremacy of the *ummah* above the nation is similarly disapproved. Even socialism is not favoured as it contradicts the faith in karma as the decisive influence in life. The Hindu view of life sees a contradiction between liberty and equality. Equality demands levelling down of liberty; some might say "dumbing down". How can one control anyone's better karma? Welfare of all, yes, but forced equality, no.

Imperialism and the exploitation of other nations are both wrong. They are equivalent to robbery. Collective unity of one's own people in order to dominate others is wrong.

Instead, the Hindu blessings are with those who strive to actualise themselves and thus bring out the best in themselves. Killing, even of animals and birds, is not desirable and the Jains particularly are sensitive to the destruction of even vegetation especially that grown below the ground. The worship of the *peepal* tree is symbolic of the Hindu respect for ecology. Most of the ills that one sees are the result of centuries of rule by others over India.

There is not a great deal of political or ideological literature. Nevertheless, Veer Savarkar first defined Hindutva or Hinduness in a single volume. It is valuable for those who wish to study the theoretical aspects of the ideology. After that came a volume called *The Saffron Book* and it is reported that a book called *The Grammar of Hindudom* is under publication. It is noteworthy that it is the only ideology which is Asia's own, unlike all other political theories which are foreign or rather European.

Ideology is essentially a Western phenomenon, just as political science is a European pre-occupation. In sharp contrast, we in India have so far to our credit only two theses on this subject: one, the famous *Arthashastra* written more than 2,500 years ago, and the second published only two years ago titled *Krishna Rajya*. Hindu India had only one history book, which was *Rajatarangini* by the Kashmiri scholar Kalhana, which again was many centuries ago.

On the other hand, European political parties are guided by their ideologies, which are many, beginning with communism on the extreme left, to what is understood as fascism on the extreme right. Take for example, Britain. Only recently, Jeremy Corbyn was an extreme socialist. Earlier, there was Aneurin

Bevan (former member of UK Parliament), who designed and implemented Britain's famous National Health Service. Harold Wilson, who was Prime Minister, had the reputation of being a leftist. Comparatively, Clement Attlee was a middle-of-the-road politician, while his contemporary Hugh Gaitskell was looked upon as a liberal. Yet, all these men belonged to the Labour Party.

On the Conservative Party side, Sir Anthony Eden was a rightist and went to war against Egypt in 1956 over the Suez Canal. Later, Margaret Thatcher was a right-winger and anti-socialist. Yet earlier, there was Enoch Powell who declared "Rivers of blood will flow in England as a result of immigration". Even fascism, considered right extremism, did not spare British politics. Sir Oswald Mosley, a son-in-law of Lord Curzon, openly admitted to being a fascist. Despite all these differences in ideology, leaders, even eminent ones, occasionally did change their parties. Winston Churchill, who was looked upon as a diehard conservative, had for a few years crossed over to the Liberal Party.

Was our Constitution a Compromise Document?

ON 16 NOVEMBER 2020, while celebrating the anniversary of the adoption of the Indian Constitution, Lok Sabha Speaker Om Birla dutifully lauded our national document for providing everyone the right to equality. It was understandably not the occasion to recount what is the reality in practice. With the advent of the Hindu Code Bill in 1955, polygamy was abolished but not for all men. The Sharia continued to be in vogue, which allowed some men to have four wives at a time. When the Constitution permits the practice of two laws in one country, how can there be equality? Article 44 did provide for a uniform civil code to be framed but little has been done so far.

Rather similarly, Article 30 gives a special right to all minorities for setting up and running educational institutions freely whereas the majority community is required to seek the consent of the prescribed authorities. Since the Right to Education was passed in 2009, all schools, except the minority ones, must teach 25 percent children of economically weaker sections without charging fees. Why not also the minority run schools?

If there was no hurry, why was the Government of India Act of 1935 used as a skeleton for framing the Constitution and various other articles added later? The 1935 Act was passed by the British Parliament for governing its Indian empire more effectively and not for developing a free country. If the British laws were satisfactory, someone could ask as to why we asked for Independence? In the event the Constitution was a compromise between communities, why should it have been necessary on the morrow of Partition, to give the Muslims their homeland when no other minority had asked for any special concession? In any case, Muhammad Ali Jinnah had insisted that Muslims were not a minority but a nation, and he stressed his Two-Nation theory in several speeches. Moreover, as early as 1877 and 1878 at Meerut and Lucknow respectively, Sir Syed Ahmad Khan had declared that the Hindus and Muslims were separate nations.

In the course of the first fifty years of the life of the Constitution, it was amended eighty-three times and by January 2020, the total number of amendments had reached 104 passed; nearly one and a half amendment per year. The USA over 239 years has amended its Constitution only 26 times; Japan since 1945 only once. This also indicates that the Indian Constitution was finalised without sufficient time, thought and homework, or it was a compromise document, and, therefore, had to be amended frequently.

Apart from the 140 amendments proposed over the years and 104 of them passed, we have taken our Constitution lightly. Take erstwhile Articles 370 and 35A abolished a year ago, which were called temporary, passed only by the Cabinet and not even shown to the Parliament. The erstwhile Planning Commission, which was to steer the country's economic development was established by a Cabinet decision. These are only some examples which make one wonder whether a tome should not be attempted on the constitutional history of Independent India. Our national document is so often mentioned in the media, especially in television debates, more because of those who wish to overlook the Partition to duck their forefather's guilt for causing it.

Acharya Durga Das Basu (Padma Bhushan), retired judge of the Calcutta High Court, in his book on the Constitution had suggested that by the year 2000, this document should be thoroughly revised. It had been amended 83 times on a piecemeal basis over five decades. He felt that a commission should be set up with eminent experts and a comprehensive new draft should be prepared. He exhorted the commission, if and when appointed, to remember that its new draft should be suited to the problems of the Indian people and not be a slavish imitation of the West. Moreover, its 442 Articles (in 2000 AD) make it by far the longest such national document in the world.

In 1955, the Congress party resolved to introduce a socialistic pattern of society. In 1976, the 42nd amendment was passed when most leading Opposition leaders were in jail due to the Emergency. The Preamble was amended to state that India is also a "socialist republic". This was done to probably justify in 1976 the nationalisation of general insurance, large banks and the coal industry *post facto*. Without touching this Constitution or overturning socialism, in 1991, the Government of India abandoned socialism and adopted liberalisation, including globalisation as its policy. It was called 'reforms' which are still continuing. Why treat the Constitution so cavalierly? If the Constitution is found unsuitable or inconvenient, why not rely on conventions, traditions and pass an act of Parliament when necessary, as happens in Britain?

The unity of the people of India, professing numerous faiths, has been sought to be achieved by enshrining the ideal of a 'secular state', which means that the state protects all religions equally and does not itself uphold any religion as the state religion. The secular objective of the state has been specifically expressed by inserting the word 'secular' in the Preamble of the Constitution (42nd Amendment) Act, 1976. On the other hand, the liberty of 'belief, faith and worship' promised in the Preamble is implemented by incorporating the fundamental rights of all citizens relating to 'freedom of religion' in Articles 25-29, which guarantee to each individual freedom to profess, practice and propagate their religion and assure strict impartiality on the part of the state and its institutions towards all religions.

Articles 29 and 30 appear to contradict the promise of secularism in the Preamble as well as what has been written in the above paragraph. Furthermore, Article 44 states: 'The State shall endeavour to secure for the citizens a uniform civil code throughout the territory of India'. Nothing has been done towards implementing this provision of the Constitution. No one other than a Muslim can have four wives at a time. All Muslim wives have a Damocles sword hanging over their heads that they can be divorced with a notice of three months, whereas all other wives are protected against any such arbitrary treatment. This situation not only violates secularism but all provisions of equality such as Articles 15, 16 etc.

Moreover, both liberty and equality are promised in the Preamble. The majority of the citizens have faith in their karmas leading to their fate; so logically they should strive to improve their karmas. On the other hand, equality necessitates equalising their fates but how? By levelling down the karmas of some as well as pushing up the karmas of others so that equality among citizens is achieved? The introduction of socialism in the Preamble by amending Article 42 in 1976 highlights this contradiction more emphatically.

Lessons on Secularism from France

THE BIRTH OF secularism owed to what Martin Luther and John Calvin perceived as the Vatican imperialism. The situation in Europe before the age of the Reformation—which would be roughly at the beginning of the 1520s—was such that each year, three hundred thousand gold pieces had to be sent from the German-speaking areas to Rome. The reformers saw this state of affairs as of no benefit to the Germanic people. In fact, they suspected that the gold was mostly misused in luxuries, even of a carnal nature, indulged in by senior priests at the Vatican.

Nevertheless, Christianity vaguely provided the ideology for the monarchies in Europe. At the time of the 16th and 17th centuries, neither capitalism nor Marxism nor even fascism had been conceptualised. Therefore, when the French Revolution broke out in 1789, there were three houses of the National Assembly–the Lords or Counts, the Commons or the Merchants and the Abbots and Bishops. The Church owned up to a third of the farming land.

As nationalism began to provide an alternative to religion, the concept of secularism sprouted and gradually became important, and the idea that all citizens could and ought to be treated as equals began taking root. Call it an alternative theology or more accurately a non-theology, but secularism too is an Abrahamic need. All the three religions that regard Abraham as the first prophet begin with God. Thereafter they provide a detailed prescription of how to lead life and, in the early times, ended with slaves and how to treat them.

There has thus been so much of religion in the social sphere, and in Islam even in political life, that secularism was necessary to neutralise this influence of faiths and enable civil society and democracy to function. In some Islamic countries, the constitutions begin by ascribing the sovereignty to Allah the Merciful. This is the opening credo of the 1973 Constitution of Pakistan. The earlier ones, I believe, also had the same provision. How can secularism or democracy coexist in such a constitution?

"Whereas sovereignty over the entire Universe belongs to Almighty Allah alone, and the authority to be exercised by the people of Pakistan within the limits prescribed by Him is a sacred trust", is how Pakistan's Constitution begins.

Before going further, we do need to record a modern definition of secularism. The old one, which was an outcome of the age of the Reformation, was based merely on the separation of the Church from the State. Prof Bernard Stasi was commissioned by the French government of President Jacques Chirac in 2003, to report on what precisely was secularism. The last was defined in the French Constituent of 1905 when

France became a strictly secular state. We may quote Prof Stasi briefly:

(i) Freedom of conscience,

(ii) Equality in law for spiritual and religious belief, and

(iii) Neutrality of political power.

In other words, there are in any modern state, three sets of relations: (a) religion and the individual; (b) the state and the individual, and; (c) the state and religion.

The state is excluded from the relationship at (a). In the second (b), the state views the individual as a citizen and not as a member of a religious group. The implication of the third (c) is that religion and state function in two separate areas of human activity. A professor of history, Donald Smith, has compared the above relations as three sides of a triangle. And the integrity of (a) and (b) is largely determined by the third relationship which separates them. Therefore, for any state to function as a secular state, it is of the utmost importance that there is a wall of separation between the State and the Church.

The French law had attempted to implement these principles. It had not abolished the wearing of either Jewish skull caps or Muslim headscarves. All that it had ordained was that the students attending government schools or employees working in government offices must not display religious symbols of a conspicuous nature, which would include even a large cross. There is no restriction on wearing of any form of dress or display of any religious symbols in the country at large.

The state, however, has to maintain absolute neutrality between one religion and another. The French insistence on secularism or the absolute separation of the religion from the state goes back to 1905, when in December that year a

Republican Law was passed by the National Assembly. Its Article 1 assured the liberty of conscience. It guaranteed the free exercise of religious beliefs. The only restrictions were decreed in the interest of public order.

Christophe Jaffrelot (professor of Indian politics and Sociology, London), in a newspaper article in March 2020, displayed a creative memory when he claimed that it was Sir Syed Ahmad Khan who formed the Muslim League. He did nothing of the kind. What he did form was the Aligarh Muslim University. It is no use bringing him into a discussion on secularism, for in 1887 and 1888 in his speeches at Meerut and Lucknow respectively, he declared that Hindus and Muslims were separate nations. Sir Syed was exclusively a Muslim leader. In the summer of 1906, 35 eminences led by Sir Aga Khan formed a delegation to submit a memorandum before the Viceroy at Shimla. In continuation, in December 1906 at Dacca (now Dhaka), the All India Muslim League was formed. To get local support, Nawab Salimullah was given a loan of £ 1000,000, oddly enough by the Viceroy. There has been nothing secular about Muslim politics either before or after Partition.

The only occasion on which some sort of a secular tune was played in Pakistan was by Qaid-e-Azam Muhammad Ali Jinnah on 11 August 1947, in his address to the Constituent Assembly. He said Hindus, Muslims and others could pray freely but henceforth, they all were Pakistanis first. If one is supposed to believe this, one has every right to ask—pray, what was the rationale for demanding and rioting for a separate state for Muslims?

Origin of Dynastic Parties

UNTIL S NIJALINGAPPA was the President of Indian National Congress (INC), the party was professional, led by a galaxy of leaders. The Congress in West Bengal was headed by Atulya Ghosh. There was Chandrabhan Gupta in Uttar Pradesh, Sachchidananda Sinha in Bihar, Biju Patnaik in Orissa, Neelam Sanjiva Reddy in Andhra Pradesh, Yashwantrao Chavan in Maharashtra, Morarji Desai in Gujarat and K Kamraj in Tamil Nadu.

Following the death of President Zakir Husain, there followed a presidential election. Neelam Sanjiva Reddy was proposed by the Congress as its candidate. Indira Gandhi did not agree and informally encouraged VV Giri to stand as an independent candidate. The Congress leaders called the Syndicate by the press did not approve of Indira's irregular behaviour. The voting that followed went in favour of Giri, who became the President of India. From the viewpoint of the Congress party, this was tantamount to the grossest indiscipline.

They, therefore, expelled her from the party. Prime Minister Indira Gandhi called her group of MPs and other followers of the Congress R (Ruling) and with the support of the Communist parties in the Lok Sabha, continued to be the prime minister. The rest of the Congressmen, led by the Syndicate, called themselves the Congress O (Organisation). The structure of the party, the real estate and various committees like the PCCs and DCCs remained with the organisation. For a year or two, members, whether senior or junior, continued to cross sides. Mostly the flow was from Congress O to Congress R.

The Congress (R) continued to be in power until March 1977; then came the post-Emergency election which reduced the ruling Congress to 160 seats, won mostly from the South. The Hindi heartland sent only two members to the Lok Sabha, one from Chhindwara in Madhya Pradesh and another from Rajasthan. The Congress then ceased to be Ruling and called itself the Congress (K), initial of K Brahmananda Reddy, ex-chief minister of Andhra Pradesh. Over the months, Indira Gandhi let it be known that she would like to be the president of the party; without this privilege, she could not carry on. This issue was discussed at length during the December 1977 AICC meeting. The majority answer was negative. The meeting ended on the 31st of the month. Before leaving the hall, she let it be known that she would be available at the Glass House, which was well-known in Bangalore. Four AICC members followed her there; two of them being the late Kamalapati Tripathi and Subrata Mukherjee, who is at present a cabinet minister in West Bengal.

It was soon announced in the press that a new party had taken birth, and was named the Congress (I). In due course, the

Congress (K) members began walking across to the Congress (I). A few who differed formed their own camp, one example being the Congress (Socialist).

In 1978, Indira Gandhi contested a by-election to the Lok Sabha from the Chikmagalur constituency in Karnataka. The election was well managed, especially with the help of Chief Minister Devaraj Urs. Her opponent was Veerendra Patil of the Janata Party who had earlier been chief minister of the state. By 1979, rumours had started flying about the future of the Janata Party government. It was rumoured that Indira Gandhi's son Sanjay was maneuvering Chaudhary Charan Singh and his supporters to bring down the Morarji Desai government, which eventually fell on 28 July 1979. It was replaced by a government led by Charan Singh, supported from the outside by the Congress. The new prime minister did not have the confidence to face the Lok Sabha. Fresh elections had to be called before the end of six months, which brought Indira Gandhi back to power, with Sanjay Gandhi as her de facto deputy, although officially he represented only the Amethi constituency.

Hardly anyone had the courage to complain openly, although many whispered about there being family rule. In retrospect, there is no doubt that between Indira Gandhi and her son Sanjay, a dynastic tradition had been introduced in the Congress and soon enough, this contagion spread to other political parties. Very sadly, in June 1980, Sanjay Gandhi crashed near the Safdarjung airport in Delhi while flying a two-seater aircraft. Thereafter, for quite a while, it was believed that Indira Gandhi's preoccupation was to somehow persuade her elder son Rajiv, who was then an Indian Airlines pilot, to join the Congress and thus replace Sanjay. She did eventually succeed and in May 1981, Rajiv contested a by-election from his deceased brother's Amethi constituency.

Although Rajiv was not politically savvy, he began dabbling in the Congress affairs as much as he could. He was soon designated general secretary; the message was that he was Party President Indira's number two. He did not have aptitude for politics, but the party flatterers saw to it that he enjoyed the pomp and glory of his office. Many a Congressman could see the blunders Rajiv was making, and some even whispered their fears. For example, in Gujarat, the Congress had been looked upon as the most Leftist party but Rajiv Gandhi, with his behaviour, as well as what he wore gave a contrarian impression. His Ray-Ban glasses, Gucci footwear and fancy watches all gave the impression of a young, handsome man overflowing with wealth. A number of Congressmen remarked in private that their party was earlier referred to by the common folk as *apni* party–our party. That popular impression would soon die, they feared. There was general agreement on one point, and that was that Rajiv's demeanor was that of an archetypal *yuvaraj* (crown prince) of India.

Then, the assassination of Indira Gandhi on 31 October 1984 shocked the nation. By 11 am, BCC Radio news confirmed that she was no more. Yet, the All India Radio as well as Doordarshan merely reported that she had been shot at by her security guard and moved to the AIIMS Hospital. This report was repeated until 6 pm in the evening. By then, President Zail Singh as well as Rajiv Gandhi had managed to reach the Rashtrapati Bhavan; the former from West Asia and the latter from West Bengal. Rajiv was sworn in as prime minister without him being elected as the leader of the Congress

Parliamentary Party. Such was the power of the dynasty, which ignored even a statutory election.

In 1991, Rajiv Gandhi was assassinated at Sriperumbudur in Tamil Nadu. There was no readymade heir. His children, Rahul and Priyanka, were too young. The search began for the weakest but acceptable substitute. Rajiv's widow Sonia Gandhi's choice fell on PV Narasimha Rao, who had retired. Most of his baggage had already reached Andhra Pradesh and he had no record of popularity. That Rao turned out to be such a capable and decisive person was a subsequent bolt from the blue. That was sufficient for Sonia Gandhi to feel insecure and take the reins in her hands. The 2004 and 2009 general elections were fought under her leadership with Dr Manmohan Singh being given the power of attorney as prime minister. Rahul Gandhi had entered politics but did not seem to have the confidence to handle a single portfolio in the ministry. Yet, as favourite *babalog*, he and his sister could tear to pieces the PM's public policy statement.

The Congress had dominated Indian politics so much and for so long that other political parties now appeared to have caught the fever of dynasty, for better or worse. In the north, there are the Akalis, the Samajwadis in UP, the Lalu clan in Bihar and the TMC in Bengal, which seem afflicted by the same malaise lately. The south is also not free of this bug, with the DMK and the Gowda Janata Dal being examples. Coming to Maharashtra, we have the Shiv Sena and Sharad Pawar's NCP. Whither Indian democracy?

Fallout of Dynastic Parties

IN MAY 1981, a friend of mine and I spent four days in the Amethi parliamentary constituency. Rajiv Gandhi was the Congress candidate. This was earlier late Sanjay Gandhi's electoral base. Rajiv dressed in *khadi* with a Gandhi *topi* and a few speeches learnt by heart was going around systematically.

On the third day of our driving around, we came across a dhaba and stopped to have a cup of tea. Some seventeen odd men were chatting enthusiastically and we joined in. They seemed all praise for Rajiv. What good Hindi, how eloquently he speaks and how handsome he looks! At the end of the praise, I politely asked: 'What has he done for our country and society to deserve being an MP except flying Indian Airlines planes efficiently?' An old man who had said little until now suddenly piped up and asked me: 'What is troubling you with Rajiv learning his mother's vocation? Lawyers bequeath the practices to their sons and daughters; doctors their dispensaries, their hospitals. Do you object to that? Here Rajiv will have to win over the public every five years.'

The old man in Amethi had a point. I did not mention that business houses and large companies are inherited by the sons although their families do not always hold more than say 20 percent shares. There are serious disadvantages to a dynasty. It shuts out many able and aspiring politicians from rising to their level of ability and popularity. In fact, the dynastic head of the party exploits the followers. A dynastic structure, besides exploiting, automatically prevents the other politicians from growing to their fullest potential. The party also loses commensurately as the tales of exploitation and frustration spread. Young aspirants begin avoiding or leaving the party.

Most people, especially in their youth, are choosey about the party's ideology. Some would rather avoid a communist party or what they perceive as a communal party. In the bargain the political sphere of the country would shrink and gradually move it to one or two monopolistic parties. And that would begin to push out democracy.

Democracy has much more to it than merely giving people freedom. Without it the civilizational growth of the country is unlikely. It also helps to throw up leaders from the different corners of society; a dictatorship does not. In China, for example, one has to go up only through the Communist Party.

One of the causes, and an important one, for the end of the Soviet Union has been ascribed to the lack of democracy and regular elections. There was no feedback from the ground about the Kremlin. It was alleged that the leaders in the Kremlin did not know what was happening in the farms and the factories. It shows how callous the leaders were and also there was a great deal of truth in this allegation. Coming back to India, until early 1977, Indira Gandhi did not know how the public in north India hated the Emergency. The secret agencies thought it was alright to hold elections and they turned out to be a disaster.

We have seen the disadvantages of dynastic political parties but when it comes to the privatisation of PSUs there is no reluctance to sell any of the units to dynastic business houses. The same logic applies to business as to politics. And the effect on the country's wealth is worse when a generation or two later the house collapses. The government may not incur a loss but the country does lose out.

Vision, management and integrity are not passed from father to son to grandson. The insolvency law introduced by this government will expose who is what in terms of their financial management. Many business houses would have already put their house in order, while those who could not, could go insolvent.

One can take it for granted that most of the losses are attributable to dishonesty of those who borrowed irresponsibly or those who lent similarly. These factors are well-known. What is different is the psychology behind them. An ancient Indian tradition has been that a father would teach the secrets of his vocation only to his sons. As a result, the secrets, if valuable, do not benefit the rest of society. This means that dynastic mentality runs in our genes. The result of these genes is that the society, as a whole, loses out completely when a family runs out of its special secret knowledge.

Indian companies do not grow large enough unlike American corporations. The latter are allowed to grow with professionals as the managers. The owners look after their investment in their companies only. A time comes when the family may have only five or ten percent shares and no control; yet business progresses well.

There is a particular reason for this efficiency. If any other company thinks that there is considerable scope of improving the performance of corporation X, it may offer to buy up to 100 percent shares of X. If the offer is distinctly much higher than the prevailing quotation for its shares on the Stock Exchange, it is best for the Directors of X to accept the offer and get out. In short, in the USA and some other countries like the UK, the directors of all corporations must run them efficiently to avoid this threat of a takeover.

One worrying issue for our country is the weakening of the Opposition. There have been comments at home and abroad which allege that in India democracy is dying. One overseas agency has gone to the extent of stating that India is moving towards an electoral autocracy. It is not that there are no effective parties opposing the BJP, which has lost elections in the three states of West Bengal, Tamil Nadu and Kerala. There is the Pawar Congress, the Shiv Sena, the Samajwadi and the BSP in UP and a variety of Janata Dals. The worrying part is that none of them has a modern manifesto relevant for the next decade.

The Samajwadi party is based on an alliance of Muslims and Yadavs. The BSP is essentially Dalit-based. The Janata Dals hark back to what late Dr Ram Manohar Lohia said which made sense in his day, that in India caste is class. The DMK in Tamil Nadu has confirmed its attachment to a dynasty by Chief Minister Stalin enabling his son Udhayanidhi Stalin to become an MLA. The Trinamool Congress has also joined the Dynasty club with its leader treating her young nephew Abhishek as her number two. The Congress is a strange phenomenon; many of its senior members feel that they have no future nor does the Party have prospects. They suffer and protest but do not leave. Perhaps they are used to the idea of its top leadership being dynastic. Since Gandhi became the unchallenged leader it has been so; Nehru, Indira, Rajiv and Sonia Gandhi. Rahul and Priyanka are ready after Sonia.

What could be the explanation for so many parties turning dynastic? Could it be due to the old Hindu tradition of a father invariably passing on his knowledge and secrets only to his favourite son? One of the reasons ascribed for the decline and virtual downfall of a great science like Ayurveda was this narrowness in spreading its knowledge and encouraging its research and development. A science that represented the concept of not only curing the sick but also making the healthy healthier.

Owaisi and 2022 UP Elections

ANXIETIES OVER THE threatened advent of Asaduddin Owaisi's All India Majlis Ittehadul Muslimeen (AIMIM) are causing more political tremors than perhaps justified. The last event was the proposal approach by the Congress to the maulana of Furfura Sharif, who is a popular leader in his area. As has been reported earlier, Owaisi had stated during his visit to West Bengal that he had tied up with Furfura for fighting the forthcoming assembly elections.

Some observers felt that Mamata Banerjee was also worried about a Hyderabad invasion cutting her votes. Owaisi's apparent creditability in eastern India is owed to his party's win in five assembly seats in the recent Bihar assembly polls. In these polls, Owaisi also gained a reputation for being a greater *vote katwa* than a winner (a vote katwa is one who weakens another candidate by cutting into his vote bank or support base). No matter the defeat of MIM in West Bengal, it is Uttar Pradesh in 2022 where Owaisi would be revealed to be a true lion, or merely a regional mouse. Whether his presence achieves a communal polarisation in India's largest state, as happened in 1937, will be known soon enough. Within three years of that provincial election, MA Jinnah brought forth the Pakistan Resolution at Lahore.

If Owaisi achieves a big divide, it would be a matter of great challenge to all political parties in the country. For the BJP, the challenge could also be a great opportunity to divide the Muslim vote—Shia-Sunni versus Ahmediya Muslims, *mardana* (men) versus *janana* (women), a common civil code, especially the abolition of polygamy. Plus, the BJP could publicise the pathetic post-independence history of Pakistan and how badly Islamabad has treated the Balochs and the Sindhis. Nevertheless, following Owaisi's AIMIM is like asking for a reverse CAA law.

For the self-styled secular parties, the threat posed by Owaisi is more immediate. MIM speakers would argue that they are at the exclusive service of their Muslim brethren. Other than them, MIM has nobody else to cater to. The Samajwadi Party has Yadavs and other voters to look after. The Bahujan Samaj Party has Dalits to lead. The Trinamool Congress has more Hindus to cater to than Muslims. Similar is the case with parties like the Telangana Regional Samiti (TRS), Sharad Pawar's NCP and the CPM.

The Congress has always claimed that it represents every segment of Indian society. This has been so since the days of Gandhi. In any case, Muslims have been voting for the Congress for six decades, Owaisi would argue, but what has the community gained from it? We are a less-educated society; some would say rather backward and certainly less well-off.

This has been the community's refrain since the 1952 elections and continues to be so.

If Muslims vote only for the AIMIM, their identity would be secure. The community can, of course, ask the party to provide schools and hospitals and also expect jobs. Owaisi can forcefully argue that his party has succeeded in convincing a section of the Muslim *qaum* to not only vote for it, but also enable it to win seats in last year's Bihar elections. However, he failed to make an entry in West Bengal in the state's assembly elections this year.

In opposition to MIM, the secular parties might contend that the MLAs of the MIM would be insufficient to form governments. What then would its five MLAs from Bihar do? It will be the same story again and again. Janab Owaisi might feel pleased, but what about those who vote for his party? However, the threat of polarisation posed by Owaisi and his party is real.

It would perhaps be no exaggeration to state that more than Bihar or Bengal, Owaisi's real target is Uttar Pradesh, India's largest and politically most important state, which is to go to the polls in March next year. The BJP not only dominates the state politically but headed by Yogi Adityanath, has been unequivocal about its Hinduness, which also sees assertive expression from time to time. On the other hand, there is a sense of angst among the Muslims at having lost the political veto they held over the state's politics during the 'secular' heyday of Congress and Samajwadi rule. A good showing by Owaisi's AIMIM in Bihar, Bengal or elsewhere might have just been the green light that segments of the community are looking for.

It is, of course, easy to dismiss such reasoning as alarmist. But one mustn't forget that in the 1937 provincial elections held across India following the passing of the Government Act of 1935, a near-defunct Muslim League not only came back into the political reckoning strongly, but within just five years, by 1942, had become the sole spokesperson of the subcontinent's Muslims. The road to Partition, thereafter, is well-known.

Significantly, the Muslim League itself fared poorly in the 1937 provincial elections. But the Congress, which claimed to be sole spokesperson for all Indians fared very badly in the Muslim seats of the United Provinces (as Uttar Pradesh was then known). Of the sixty Muslim seats in UP, the Congress contested nine but did not win a single one. However, its spectacular performance in the general seats enabled it to form provincial governments, as it now had comfortable legislative majorities of its own. Earlier commitments of incorporating the Muslim League were soon dumped. In UP for example, the Congress agreed to include some leaders of the Muslim League into the government only if they agreed to dissolve the Muslim League in UP and merge themselves into the Congress. The League in no mood to commit political suicide naturally refused. It now turned increasingly and firmly to Jinnah as its only saviour.

More significantly, Jinnah and the Muslim League used the 1937 elections to portray the Congress as a Hindu-only party. The perception was successfully utilised in galvanising Muslim masses and political leaders in Punjab and Bengal. The prospect of de-colonization and the thought of an India under Congress, i.e., Hindu rule was anathema to them. They realised they needed a leader and forceful negotiator to advance their interests, which Jinnah repeatedly told them could be guaranteed only by the carving out of a separate state for themselves based on religious identity.

Arguably, the UP and India of 2022 are very different from 1937. But the intransigence of a particular community and political leaders waiting to exploit it are eerily similar.

Admittedly, the signs are not reassuring. No one in his or her right mind can even contemplate another partition along religious lines as a solution to this polarised existence. The times of the 1930s and 1940s were different; the majority community, then in awe of Gandhi, went out of its way to seek accommodation with others. But with the majority having turned assertive and stridently nationalist, any talk of a vivisection would be tantamount to asking for civil war.

Clearly, the onus of taking a moderate path is squarely upon the religious minorities. No nation or modern polity can survive, leave alone prosper by continually caving in to obscurantist religious demands, which only invite backlash and are counter-productive to those indulging in it. Muslims are thus in need of genuinely moderate leaders and organisations which will lead them out of the dark fantasies of failed and destructive ideas and enable them to march lockstep with progress and modernity.

Misuse of Rajya Sabha

AS ARTICULATED IN many journals and publications, many people have voiced from time to time, doubts about the utility of the upper house of legislature whether in the States or at the Centre. The cause of these doubts is the frequent misuse of the Rajya Sabha as well as the Vidhan Parishads. With the growth of Sanjay Gandhi's influence in the 1970s, more of his friends were lifted into the upper house of Parliament. Fortunately for them, the election rule-framers prescribed the minimum age for the candidates chosen for Rajya Sabha as 30. Hence, the only restriction was that, like for the Lok Sabha (25 years), anyone who had completed 30 years was eligible to enter the upper house. In many ways, this was the original cause of misuse.

The upper house was never meant for the young Indian woman or man to get into. For they, being young and fit, could cultivate the common folk, build bases for the party and in due course contest a Lok Sabha seat. The young and raw individuals contributed very little to the quality of debates or to the Parliament. The purpose of the upper house, whether at the Centre or the States was that older mature individuals, preferably well-educated could devote time to study issues and then speak on them in an educated manner. They may or may not relate to the common folk of a constituency nor the mass voters relate to them.

The upper house should be used to accommodate leaders who can make competent ministers and have to get elected within six months of their appointment by the prime minister or a chief minister. One recent example is that of Yogi Adityanath. He was in the Lok Sabha when the UP assembly elections were held in 2017 and he had not contested an MLA seat. Yet, he was selected to be chief minister and, therefore, had to enter the assembly. He could have requested an MLA to give up his seat and the Yogi could have got himself into the assembly. Instead of doing that, he chose not to disturb anyone; there was a Vidhan Parishad seat vacant which he used to come into the assembly to remain qualified to be a minister. When in 2001 Narendra Modi was in a similar situation in Gujarat, he could not do the same. There being no Vidhan Parishad in his state, Modi had to get elected from an assembly seat vacated by an MLA.

Having been a member of Rajya Sabha, I found that the level of debates and discussions were, on the whole, more sober and mature than those in the Lok Sabha. Generally, the speakers in the upper house said that they had studied and reflected on the subject they spoke on, whereas in the Lok Sabha, more members spoke off-the-cuff. Many of them regularly left Delhi on Friday afternoons, if not on Thursday evenings, to return on Monday mornings. The Rajya Sabha members could afford to spend the weekends in Delhi and read up before speaking the following week.

The communist parties had a commendable system; most of their upper house members mostly spent the weekends in Delhi. They not only studied the current subjects but also collected the anticipated bills coming up for debate and passed on their notes to their Lok Sabha colleagues. I offered to organise a small secretariat at my cost for all my party members so that all of us could be better prepared for speaking at discussion time. Being in power after long years and with a lenient leadership, the general mood in the party was one of overconfidence. Little wonder that the 2004 general election was lost on a manifesto which projected "India Shining". For every shining Indian, there were many more lesser fortunate citizens who were not.

In India, our constituencies are large and the voters are much more varied than say in the Western countries. Moreover, our diversity makes it useful for members of Parliament and even assemblies to know other parts of the country. The upper house members would have the leisure to do this kind of work during the weeks when their house does not sit. Members of the lower house cannot normally have so much leisure; their focus has to be on their own voters. If the legislators do not take their knowledge seriously, they would yield helplessly to the dominance of the executive or the Ministers.

It is for the political parties to realise and decide whether they wish to make serious use of the upper house or exploit it for their convenience. But truly these chambers can be useful as knowledge-cum-wisdom banks for not only the parties but also for the country. They can help to raise the quality of politics.

Getting elected by lakhs of people is related to popularity or at least acceptability, whereas knowledge depends on education and experience. Both are necessary virtues; the lower house is more for the party, while the upper house more for the country in the long run, if used wisely.

China's Border Claims

THE UNITED STATES Congress has passed a Tibet Policy and Support Act that says the choice of the next Dalai Lama is the prerogative only of Tibetans. In addition, any attempt by the Chinese to interfere in the Dalai Lama's succession would result in sanctions against that country. Lobsang Sangay, the Prime Minister of Tibetan government-in-exile has already made his first visit to Washington DC. It is almost certain that China will not sit quiet on the American action. But then controversy is the spice of politics. It is likely that sanctions lead to counter-action and so on.

India need not do anything publicly but, at the same time, should respect the seniority and holiness of the Dalai Lama if he declares his successor. He may address his country's young men and women to tell them to come across to India if they are not happy where they are. He knows there will be employment for them. Let us face it—until 1951, China had no ongoing suzerainty over Tibet. During the rule of the Manchus over

China, the Sino-Tibetan relations were cordial, so much so that in 1728, the Chinese imperial troops helped to quell a civil war in Tibet. When Tibet had to face wars with Ladakh in 1842 and with the Gurkhas in 1858, however, the Manchus could not help. What kind of suzerainty was that?

To clear all claims of Manchus to overlordship, Tibet in 1912 expelled all the Chinese from their land and declared Tibetan independence as a republic. It was only in October 1950 that the Chinese invaded eastern Tibet. In 1951, Peking (new Beijing) dictated a treaty with Lhasa. It was an open act of aggression and it was unfortunate that India recognised it out of ignorance as well as leftist sympathies for Communist China. If the matter goes to the International Court of Justice at The Hague, the only piece of paper that China can produce before the court is a treaty with Britain in 1904 which recognised Chinese suzerainty over Tibet without Lhasa being a participant at all. Who was Britain to sell out Tibetan sovereignty? The *Encyclopedia Britannica* confirms this fact.

"All power grows out of the barrel of a gun", said Chairman Mao Zedong decades ago. Thus, he declared to the world how dear the gun was to him. One would, however, have presumed that as a responsible statesman he did not mean to announce that China was a big bully. Nevertheless, the yellow giant has hardly any friend or ally beyond North Korea and Pakistan. Mao Zedong did not spare even the superpower Soviet Union; in 1960 began the quarrel with Moscow, according to Neville Maxwell, a former South Asia correspondent of *The Times*, London. Peking (now Beijing) began by accusing Nikita Khrushchev, the General Secretary of the Soviet Communist Party of being a revisionist soon after the 1959 revolt in Tibet.

Peking felt that ideologically the correct thing to do was for the Soviets to support it rather than New Delhi.

Soon thereafter, tension began on the banks of the Ussuri River, which traditionally marked the frontier of Russia in Asia. The tension escalated until in March 1969, it exploded into the Battle of Zhenbao Island on the river. Across is the Xinjiang province of China where are concentrated the Muslim Uyghurs. Although the Soviet Union was loaded with a nuclear arsenal, Mao Zedong was confident that a large number of men can overwhelm a weaponised enemy. Human power, at its best and largest, would be decisive over economic power plus armaments. Reportedly, the Politburo in Moscow was apprehensive of a mass invasion into Soviet territory; there is still very much a possibility that it may take place. China has people without space while Russia has land space without people. What an extraordinary contrast between neighbours! Each can fit into the other.

Yet in 1968, the Soviet Union had nearly four hundred thousand soldiers and 1,200 aircraft on its border while China reportedly had deployed a million and a half troops on its frontier. In the 1969 Battle of Zhenbao, about a hundred soldiers were killed and approximately 300 were wounded. One has to imagine the Chinese gumption to be aggressive against a nuclear power who could then have wiped out a large portion of the yellow giant.

Russia and India are not the only countries with whom China has had border disputes. It is fair to say that if you think of disputes, do not forget China, which has claims on 16 neighbours and near-neighbours. We have seen how large countries like India and Russia have been targets. On the other hand, even small nations like Brunei, Kyrgyzstan and Laos are also not outside China's fishing net of disputes. As someone put it, in the event if ever China intrudes eastern Russia, perhaps Vladivostok, Beijing will lay claim to Alaska because once upon a time it belonged to the Czarist Empire.

Believe it not, from time to time, China claims that North Korea is a part of the yellow giant. However, until it exercises its claim, the neighbour continues to be a faithful ally. Taiwan was earlier called the Formosa Island which, upon its defeat, Japan was made to hand over to the locals. On the Maoists taking over mainland China, Chiang Kai-shek's Kuomintang party members and other followers sailed across and took refuge on the island. Historically, it was first visited by the Portuguese, then the Dutch and later by the Spaniards. Later also came some Chinese refugees from the Ming dynasty to the mainland and similarly came some Manchus. In 1895, after the Sino-Japanese war, the island was ceded to Japan. Yet today's China claims Taiwan's ownership; fortunately because of its own development as well as its armed forces supported by the USA, the latter has remained independent.

China shares a land border of 1,300 km with Vietnam. It claims large parts of Vietnam on historical grounds. Both countries are also at loggerheads over Macclesfield Bank and Paracel Islands, parts of the South China Sea and the Spratly Islands. China claims parts of the East China Sea, particularly the Senkaku Islands in Japanese territory.

China and Kazakhstan share a border of some 1,700 km in China's vast northwestern province of Xinjiang, where mostly the Muslim Uyghurs live. There are unilateral claims by China on Kazakhstan territory. China claims Kyrgyzstan on the grounds that it had unfairly itself surrendered the territory to Russia in the 19th century. Tajikistan is claimed by China again on historical grounds.

China and Burma share a long border of over 2,000 km; they signed a border agreement in 1960. Yet the Burmese feel threatened from time to time. Laos has the same problem despite a border treaty signed in 1991. Mongolia has a long frontier with China of over 4,500 km and China claims the whole country on the basis of its theory of history. Over and above these claims, there are several more against Indonesia, Malaysia, the Philippines and Singapore and over parts of the South China Sea.

A Contradiction on China

THERE ARE SOME experts in India who believe that India should leave the Quad associates alone and preferably befriend China. The finest compliment we can give the yellow neighbour from the Indian point of view is that it is a neighbourly sibling. When vital interests are involved, a sibling is a person's enemy, a vicious one at that, if not worse. At an individual level, the Mughals and their wars of succession were an emphatic example. When it comes to countries, traditionally the Franco-German relationship before the European Union came into being is a useful case. Former President Trump was busy building a wall in the south of his country on the Mexican border. The Indo-Pakistan equation continues to remain as sore as it has been.

Mao Zedong defeated Chiang Kai Shek conclusively in 1949, whereas India became free two years earlier. It is difficult to think of a country's prime minister who could have endorsed the takeover of its friendly neighbour Tibet with as great an alacrity as Prime Minister Jawaharlal Nehru did. He then went on to the Bandung Conference in 1955 organised by President Sukarno of Indonesia. Nehru repeatedly took time off at the conference to introduce the Chinese foreign minister Chou en-Lai (Zhou en Lai), as though he was launching his younger brother. Nehru did not have the slightest inkling at the time that vast tracts of his country India were being misappropriated in Aksai Chin. Later, when Nehru discovered the deception, he explained to the Indian Parliament that the lost territory did not matter; it was a land where not a blade of grass grew was his reasoning. A member of parliament, Mahavir Tyagi, retorted on the floor of the Lok Sabha, that Nehru's pate where not a strand of hair grew might not matter to him but thousands of square miles of territory certainly mattered to the country. Jawaharlal Nehru continued his policy regardless until eventually China invaded India on two fronts: Ladakh in the west and NEFA (today Arunachal Pradesh) in the east. After humiliating India to its satisfaction, the Chinese army unilaterally withdrew after a month.

Since then, for all these decades, Beijing is in occupation of Indian territory. Yet India has in recent years spent billions of dollars of foreign exchange importing a great deal of goods from China including toys and even statues of Hindu deities. Due to the Shanghai imports, many of our small and medium industries have had to close down. The World Trade Organisation (WTO), one suspects, was innovated to facilitate Chinese exports, a number of which are used for espionage. Now, many countries especially in the West have begun avoiding Chinese goods. All these decades, India could not make much effort to recover its lost territory or come to any definitive agreement on some sort of a boundary settlement. It is almost a contradiction that one country trades with another on a large scale, while their frontiers reflect the status of enemies.

As if all this was not enough, some experts say that we must not depend on either the USA or Australia to fight with us and, therefore, abandon the idea of the Quad. The only associate which could fight with us is Japan. It is not realised that the Quad need not be limited; it could be extended to say Vietnam, Taiwan and South Korea in due course. Further extension could be made with the help of Indonesia and the Philippines. Every associate need not send soldiers to take the battlefield with our troops. For example, the USA could be invaluable in providing armaments and technological assistance. Incidentally, China invaded Vietnam in 1979 but suffered a defeat at the hands of Hanoi.

Earlier in the Korean War, the Chinese People's Liberation Army (PLA) participated in a big way when the Americans took the field for saving South Korea in 1952-53. At that time, the PLA showed no concern for the lives of its own soldiers, fighting as it were with men rather than weapons. An American, who later joined the diplomatic service, told me in Kolkata that the tank in which he was riding was swarmed by up to a hundred or so Chinese soldiers who climbed on to it and blocked its passage, with only rudimentary rifles. "We in the tank drove as fast as we could", he said, while narrating the incident. He had no time to look at how many Chinese perished by getting knocked down or run over.

The PLA is not China's national army like ours, but belongs to the Chinese Communist Party, for fear of an anti-party revolt. Normally, except for some specially-trained battalions, such proxy armies are not as efficient as their national counterparts.

The reason is likely to be that the priority in recruitment would be loyalty to the party and not potential military aptitude. We cannot take for granted that there would be no adverse reaction in the West to our playing "Hindi Chini Bhai Bhai" for whatever reasons. On the other hand, it is well-known that we have border disputes with China and we could be helpful to the West for the sake of Taiwan or any other issue. Even today, many a Tibetan would have greater sympathy for India than China. Some pro-Chinese experts consider the yellow giant to be the world's number one power. Surely this cannot be true, with the US economy well ahead, plus having the most advanced technology and above all, the largest nuclear arsenal.

Living in democratic India it is difficult to visualise the uncertainty, if not the insecurity, of a dictatorial country. Since there are no electoral opportunities, the regimes have to be constantly alert to the possibilities of rebellions or revolts. The PLA being a party institution and not a national one is explained by this factor. Moreover, Tibet and Xinjiang are not integral to the Han civilisation. Coming to the economy, with rapid prosperity the class profile changes, and so has been the case in China as well. With more than subsistence-level livelihood, people begin to expect some say in the affairs of their society. There is bound to be more education more thinking and more differences in opinion. A democracy can deal with such changes, but the class thinking of the latter cannot change easily.

In a democratic country the party in power can be replaced through an election. One major reason for the Soviet Union suffering an economic bust in 1991 was attributed to the Kremlin not always aware as to what was happening in different parts of its huge country. Had there been periodic elections, as in a democratic country, they would have reflected the changing situations and problems. In the case of the Soviet Union, the Kremlin knew accurately about Moscow and perhaps Leningrad, but not very much beyond. In a conversation several years ago, a Marxist in Kolkata went to great lengths to convince me that had there been regular feedback from the ground, the Soviet Union would still be flourishing. Evidently, he could not see the inherit contradiction between popular elections and a dictatorship of the proletariat!

Jobs versus Self-Employment

FOR EARNING A living, there is nothing more pleasurable than owning and running one's own enterprise. Lately, even in India, some companies give hefty pay and perks which exceed the profits of small to medium industry, business or a professional service. Nevertheless, the satisfaction of owning one's own enterprise is greater and offsets the extra income of a top job. Mind you, a chief executive of a large corporation has several advantages other than merely his pay and perks. To be able to operate on a large scale as well the potential of further expansion on a commensurate scale is itself a substantial compensation. The larger the enterprise the greater the market, and perhaps social status and influence with a large number of people reporting to the CEO. Some chief executives experience, and rightly so, a sense of power which even a medium self-owned enterprise cannot provide. Until 1980, I headed a company with no questions ever asked by the owners or the Board of Directors, which employed 25,000 persons.

The pleasure of that experience is yet to be replicated in my own business-cum-industry which has been successful. For a musician, the pleasure of playing on a grand piano far outweighs the satisfaction that a harmonium provides; although the former belongs to someone else while the latter is one's own. The harmonium would remain one's own whereas the piano could be taken away by its master any time. The pain and humiliation of it being taken away, however, would be greater than the pleasure it ever gave you. The powers exercised by a Wazir-e-Azam were often manifold, many more than the ones normally enjoyed by the Nawab. So much so that often the former began to believe that without him the *riyasat* (state) would not run.

Nevertheless, if I were born again, I would get into my own business earlier than I did in the current innings. Although I must mention that a certain discipline and method of work that a large organisation provides, a small one seldom gives. What really is business and how to make it run one learns quicker and better from an organisation which has been at it for years. Moreover, running a large set-up has its own unique technology. It is not widely known that management science or business management as a subject was begun by what an officer observed of the German army's functioning during World War I. How best to develop an effective organisation economically and then run it optimally. An example that readily comes to mind is the famous "tooth to tail ratio". Given a division of soldiers, maximise the number of fighting or firing men and the minimum number should be deployed for servicing and supporting the frontline men with rifles and machine guns. It was subsequently discovered that the British army had a ratio of 1:10, one fighting soldier to ten service supporters. In contrast, the German ratio was 1:4. This showed the waste of manpower taking place on the British side. On this criterion, the Germans were two and a half times more efficient than the British—four non-fighters to ten for a fundamental function which was fighting and killing the enemy.

Do not get the impression that I favour the army set-up as an ideal example for organising a large company. For one, I have quoted an army example of over a century ago. Secondly, in today's context the army's fighting soldiers and officers are divided into too many layers. Well-trained soldiers would require less official supervision or leadership. In contrast, small businesses require versatile men and women on their roles—persons who know how to perform more and more functions for the simple reason that the smaller the company, the less the number of persons it can afford to employ.

Looking at the world scenario of employment, only about half the employable people have jobs. The other half is self-employed. From the wealthiest entrepreneur to the humblest hawker of fruits and vegetables, all are in the category of the self-employed. If one's education has been either law or medicine or accountancy, she/he knows what to do. If one is not vocationally qualified, one could try one's hand at business. That is where youngsters who do not belong to families with business traditions can feel lost. Business Management studies enumerate theories on commerce-related subjects but they seldom lay out advice on how to set up a business if one has no previous experience. Few successful entrepreneurs write their own stories for younger beginners to learn from. Nor apparently have publishers of educational books persuaded sufficient number of entrepreneurs to fill this gap of knowledge. Only someone who has started his/her enterprise from scratch and succeeded is the needed author.

My plea is an urgent one because in the employment market now, women in significant numbers are seeking jobs which earlier were virtually monopolies of men. Earlier we had not heard of women fighter pilots in the air force; now they are there. On the other hand, the prevalence of Covid has caused a significance reduction of jobs. Will the same number of shops survive or will home deliveries replace some of them? What are likely to be the effects of work-from-home on employment? Many should be saving an hour or two on travelling time to office and back. With the growing onslaught of Zoom meetings, how would the travel and hotel business be affected? Government jobs are also feared to reduce in number.

There was no tradition of business in my family and I worked as an executive in large companies for 23 years. By pursing acquaintances in multi-national corporations, I managed to get started with contract manufacturing of their products. That line expanded and helped me to set-up small factories making and selling similar goods for myself. This is one example of how a novice can start his/her own enterprise. But one factor is certain that the person concerned has to lose his fear of insecurity.

India is proud of its business management schools which have turned out first-rate executives for companies to benefit from. It would, however, be interesting to see a survey of these schools' alumni: what percentage of them have developed their own enterprises? A laundry, a restaurant, a grocer or a *paanwala* is a business worth learning and pursuing. Everyone need not learn how to run a large company. In fact, there is a greater need and scope for smaller enterprises.

Advantages of Emigration for India

I SHARE THE general delight at the electoral success of India's diaspora in the persona of Kamala Harris.

In my interaction with citizens of other countries, in India or overseas, I have constantly felt that we are an intelligent lot of people, not merely in the sense of knowledge but also of wisdom. Given the opportunity of quality education, India would produce so many qualified citizens that it would not be able to accommodate everyone, no matter how big our economy. Emigration might not then be a major issue.

Many Indians have persistently mistaken poor education as a reason for the brain drain. Ideally, there should be guidance for those wishing to emigrate. We could call this the technology of migration. This entails learning the language and idiom of the country to which travel is desired, and elementary knowledge of that country and the way its people conduct themselves.

Such awareness would make assimilation easier and quicker. I have relatives in the USA. One of them, a medical doctor having worked only in state hospitals in Manhattan, would have met and worked with many American doctors, black or white; yet, at her house parties, I have never met anyone except Indians. Her husband worked for IBM, but that also made no difference. They lived in Scarsdale, a New York up-market suburb. These details do not speak of true assimilation.

Fortunately, Indian immigrants do not make collective demands on their host countries, unlike many others. In Switzerland, a community demanded eternal graves for the buried to be "easily identifiable" by God's representatives on Doomsday. In Belgium, animal sacrifices by a community would be done in places of worship or their homes. Municipalities who found blood flowing out into the streets introduced a rule that goats and lambs could be sacrificed only in bathroom tubs. The remains of these animals had to be packed in a green plastic bag for disposal. Immigrants cannot be offensive to the original citizens. Cooking with strong *masalas* in a white locality was found to be highly objectionable some years ago. Potential emigrants must be systematically informed to take special care in order to make their acceptance in the new country as smooth as possible.

An objectionable practice of cricket-crazy Indian and Pakistani immigrants is waving the flags of their former nationalities during cricket matches in their host country, particularly England or Australia. British or Australian whites must feel hurt, although they may not show it. But it stands to reason that their resentment would express itself through discrimination.

Traditionally in India, families expect new brides coming in to accept their new family customs in totality, and not display overt nostalgia for their parental homes. This would be a useful example for immigrants to emulate upon relocation to a new country. With the advent of globalisation and end of colonialism, India needs to not only have more overseas contacts, but also influence. One sure way is by winning the hearts of the people of those countries. Indians have another advantage over virtually all others, which is the ready spiritual potential of Hinduism. Though it is an American initiative, ISKCON has gone quite far in spreading Hindu religion. With increasing education and spread of awareness, it has become difficult for people to be confined to a single holy book that tells believers who their prophet and "only god is". Today's enlightened youth are unlikely to accept diktats unless backed by proof.

Hinduism has little compulsion; if a person believes in cause and effect, he or she can be a Hindu without abandoning his or her alternative religion. In short, acceptance of karma is sufficient to feel and be looked upon as a Hindu. Swami Vivekananda, in his short life could explain to and inspire so many in the West, which shows the worldly practicality of our spirituality.

Kamala Harris comes in at a time when America is confused, if not also divided between so-called liberals and conservatives. There are differences between those who believe that since the USA has grown with continual immigration, its gates should remain open for new people, regardless of their ethnicity.

Others feel indiscriminate immigration will threaten America's very character that has made it the world's wealthiest and strongest country. President Biden is the oldest candidate ever to be elected to office, and the focus, therefore, is more on

Vice-President Harris, than generally would be the case. She has repeatedly claimed to be black, although she looks more Indian and is married to a Jewish gentleman—an unusual combination with political implications. She is evidently intelligent and perceptive and it would be interesting to see how she rides the trapeze of politics in the next few years. Unlike the President, Kamala Harris has a long stake in the revolving kaleidoscope of US politics. Her performance in Washington would also build or un-build the Asian persona and a woman's image at the top of the country's ladder.

A Four-day Week

A PERSON I knew happened to visit Germany and one of his business stops happened to be Hamburg. He remembered that a dear university friend of his worked there. It was a Thursday when he phoned his friend who was pleasantly surprised; they chatted for three or four minutes in the course of which the friend invited the visitor for lunch on Saturday. My acquaintance could not meet his friend because he was scheduled to leave Hamburg on Friday. The moral of this little incident is that work is worship and leisure is for play and never shall the twain overlap.

This is unlikely to happen in India, where work and play are not so rigidly separate. Traditionally, Hindus have no weekly Sabbath unlike the Jews who have the Saturday, Christians the Sunday and Muslims the Friday. The Hindus have longish festivals, extended weddings and thirteen days for mourning the death of a family member. Historically, Hindus had no system of weekly holidays; one took one, two or three days off when necessary; otherwise work went on. The working day could be long or short according to convenience. If someone dropped in unexpectedly during work time one chatted with him for say half an hour, unlike in Hamburg.

More leisure for the worker was originally a demand that emanated from the communists. It was a reaction to the 19th century exploitation of the worker by compelling him or her to work for twelve hours or more every day. The wages were also low because the factories were few. What was there in life for the poor worker was a logical question on the lips of the socialist trade union leader. In his mind was the fact that the worker was not a partner and he gained nothing by working hard. The profit was mostly the factory owner's—either the State or private. If private, by working less, the worker would help in expediting the socialist revolution.

The need for increasing leisure spread from the communists to the social democrats to anyone who believed in a welfare state. For us in India, UK, after World War II and until Margaret Thatcher, is a ready reference for a welfare state. Productivity became incidental to economic life and threatening the State was not a priority; what mattered most was more pay and less work. When I discussed with factory-level trade union leaders, they were frank. I asked how could our developing economy afford the luxury of leisure? Mostly the reply was that if the industries fail, the people's revolution would come nearer.

Once Karl Marx theorised that an economy should produce just enough goods to meet the assessed demand in order to avoid recessions and slumps, the need for productivity was forgotten. So much so that hardly any steps were taken to save the Soviet economy from sinking into lower and lower productivity. The rulers in Moscow looked on while their State collapsed and scattered into 16 splinters.

In any case, in the Indian warm to hot climate conditions, thoughts of a four-day, or even a five-day week should be avoided. In fact, we get too many holidays as it is. The Centre has a list of 16 holidays annually; then the States have their own holidays. Saturdays and Sundays total up to 104 per year. With approximately a gross number of 130 days off, well over one-third of the year, the organised office sector of the country is largely on leave. None of these off days apply to the unorganised sector which is very much larger.

Unlike the West, our climate is generally warm and humid and does not lend itself to continuous work of eight or nine hours. The work has to go slow from time to time. A young CPM trade unionist at the National Tobacco factory at Agarpada, 16 km from Calcutta, remarked during a discussion, "One cannot expect a worker in Calcutta to actually produce for more than three or four hours a day". A six-day week, therefore, should help offset this disadvantage.

Despite our efforts to become a big power, many areas of our economy are developing ones or quite frankly, underdeveloped. In other words, we have fewer assets and more people, which means we have to get more out of the assets. We also have more and more people desirous of obtaining employment. The logical corollary of this problem is to keep 24×7 working hours as our goal. Without much notice, quite a number of vocations can move to two shifts with a separate set of people working the second move. Take our law courts for instance which have huge backlogs to catch up with. They could have a second shift.

The High Courts for example could begin hearings at

8 am and work till 1 pm without interruptions. At 1.30 pm, the second set of judges could occupy the benches and carry on till 6.30 pm. As far as the advocates are concerned, they would be free to choose their briefs according to their convenience.

Working hours, days, rules and the entire ethos should be redesigned on the basis of Indian conditions and not adapted from the West. So far the labour laws have been dominated by ideas set by the Industrial Disputes Act of 1947, given to India by the British on the eve of their final departure from the country. The Labour Party had come to power in 1945 all ready to introduce socialism in Britain. Over seven decades later, it is high time not only for reform but also for a complete rethink. Firstly, socialism has cut no ice in the country as a whole. Most Indians believe in karma and do not expect equality unlike the Abrahamic religions which are embarrassed by inequality. In any case, communism perished thirty years ago except in a few spots on the globe.

What India requires broadly are systems of contracts at most levels of work, including for government officers. The conditions laid out would vary for the type and level of work but one rule should be absolutely sacred. When the pay packet is given at the end of the month, an additional 25 percent with the help of a public sector bank draft payable at the end of five years, must also be given to the employee. This would be her or his PF, gratuity etc. all in all, so that the employee is assured of post-work dues. At present, many employees are in a precarious situation. Many employers have not deposited their Provident Fund money, including cash deducted from the employee's salary.

Essentially, so long as both parties agree, contracts should be valid but their enforcement must be strict, which does not always happen in our country. And the courts adjudicating disputes should be impartial. Until now, most labour court judges have been soft in the worker's favour; sometimes excessively so, which lead to appeals that often hurt the employer.

Go Public, Rather Than Privatise

IN INDIA, IT is better to go public, fundamentally because we do not have a sufficient number of entrepreneurs with enough wealth to pay for PSUs. Many corporate houses, although efficient, have already borrowed more than ideally desirable, which explains why the government's privatisation plans have so far been behind schedule. At this stage a brief look at history would be useful.

At Independence in 1947, India had many more traders than industrialists. Take the textile mills, of which India had a fairly large number. How many have survived? With most mills the problem was with the weaving looms; they were outdated and needed to be changed. Alternatively, the mills could be trifurcated into three—carding/spinning, weaving and finishing/packing. Instead, they carried on as long as possible and when they could not the owners surrendered to closure. The National Textile Corporation (NTC) inaugurated the expansion of what could be called the hospital sector of industry; it was not really public sector although the bureaucrats chose to mix up the two.

When the NTC could not absorb more sick mills, they were allowed to wind up, sell their fixed assets including the land, pay the employee dues, and then compensate the shareholders. New hotels, office buildings or residential flats have come up on the graves of the wound-up mills. Yet the people continue to dress well, better than before. Spinners, new weavers called power looms and finishers are functioning profitably in place of many of the expired mills. This industrial tragedy is one reflection of the industrial limitations of some of our entrepreneurs.

On the other hand, there were business houses which were functioning laudably well but their hands and legs were tied down by Nehruvian socialism also vigorously practised by Indira Gandhi. Her plea was that the only way of co-existence for the rich and the poor was socialism. Apart from clamping down on business growth with a Monopolies Commission and such laws, she nationalised 19 banks, the entire coal industry as well as general insurance. Little did she realise that the whole public sector represented state capitalism and not socialism at all. It could have socialism provided the common people were given an opportunity to invest and obtain dividends. Even according to Karl Marx, socialism was "from each according to his ability to each according to his opportunity".

Thus Indian businessmen were denied the scope to grow and mature into industrialists. Those who did so, managed to set up small and medium industries by even over-borrowing from the nationalised banks. Prime Minister Narasimha Rao did a yeoman's service to the economy by liberalising the procedures and abolishing many of the restrictions. But in his quest to get re-elected for another five years, he went very easy on his reforms in the second half of his first term as PM. If one looks at his years in power, he did more for India politically than economically. Ayodhya was his biggest achievement and the first step in national revival in centuries.

Keeping all the Indian conditions in mind, the PSUs which the government desires to privatise should be managerially toned up. Only industrial managers can do that and not bureaucrats. If they are structurally imbalanced, some of them may have to be merged with other suitable PSUs. The treatment of toning up would differ from unit to unit. The toned-up ones should offer one or more public issue of shares as per SEBI and stock exchange rules. So long as the Indian state retains at least 40 percent shares, let the public have the rest of the shares. Many individuals have savings which they wish to invest but do not find avenues to do so. So on debt instruments, the interest rates have fallen so low that they are unattractive.

Let us clarify that most of our bureaucrats, IAS and others, are first-rate administrators but they are unlikely to be effective managers. The former are primarily wedded to rules and procedures whereas the latter's priorities are decisions, production and profits. The two cultures are quite distinct. Therefore, a PSU managing director should not be reporting to a bureaucrat but his shareholders. The solution lies in the President of India parting with the shares of all PSUs to financial institutions like the LIC, GIC (General Insurance Corporation) and its subsidiaries, banks, Unit Trust of India, etc. When this happens, these new holders would behave like investors and not zamindars. Moreover, politicians would no longer have ready access to recommend their candidates, use their guest houses, cars, etc. The PSUs would then operate like businesses and industries and not like jagirdaries.

If for nothing else, for taking share investments in companies from the panelled offices of the upper classes to the masses, the late Dhirubhai Ambani needs to be honoured. The best way to do so was to make the public his partners in preference to banks. His logic was that loans cost interest, shares do not. Shares compel the management to perform and deliver lucrative dividends, which is what Indians expect of the PSUs. Karl Marx believed that religion is the opium of the masses. It can be that loans are the opium of the classes.

The public sector was started because on the morrow of Independence there were few entrepreneurs who had capital for mega projects. Moreover, for a private company to take on infrastructural projects required boldness. Another factor was Jawaharlal Nehru's fascination with what he saw on his visit to the Soviet Union in the pre-Independence days. Moreover, he liked to be known as a Fabian socialist. If one wished to be seen as an anti-imperialist in those early years, one had to prefer to be seen as a socialist rather than anything else. These factors helped luxury hotels, airlines and state trading for exports to slip into the public sector. As time went on, exports of fruits and others items also were included as they fascinated some influential bureaucrat. Someone liked the cool air of Ooty and, therefore, an ophthalmologic glass factory was built, incidentally housed in an elegant building. The officer-in-charge of the public enterprises, especially for selecting executives, told me that in the early 1980s he would recommend to the government (when the units touched a total of 300) that there would be no more until profits were made by most of the PSUs.

Profit was not included in the PSU lexicon because the prime minister did not like the word. Another IAS officer said to me, 'Just see the quality of educated men we have in the public sector. Compare them with the private sector executives'. He was right. I had known a Kolkata executive who wore a dhoti and had started in the group as a *sarkar*—higher than a peon and lower than a clerk. He was allowed by the controlling family to create one of largest groups of tea gardens. 'How ridiculous', my IAS acquaintance exclaimed.

Losses overall were mounting but what were individual citizens to do? Prime Minister Lal Bahadur Shastri was in office for one and a half years; this was too short a time to do anything. In early 1966, Indira Gandhi took office and some people had hopes; she had no ideological hang-ups and ought to have been practical. But as it happened, she distrusted most politicians and certainly had greater faith in her bureaucratic advisors led by PN Haksar. On a visit to Kolkata, she happened to talk to some industrialists who had heard rumours of the coming nationalisation. Reportedly she said that in our primarily poor country, socialist policies were the only bridge to keep the poor, the rich and the middle class together.

After splitting the Congress in 1969 and having to contest a general election in 1972, meanwhile depending on the Communists to survive as prime minister, Mrs Gandhi had to fire the mass imagination. The nationalisation of banks proved the fieriest of all her economic moves. A rising entrepreneur of cosmetics came to buy my Kolkata house as I was shifting to Delhi. He said he felt very indebted to Indira's bank nationalisation. Without that, he said he could not get overdrafts from the owners of private banks. He hoped to become an honest *crorepati* on the back of nationalised banks. And in twenty years he did make it; his definition of honesty I did not check with him. The coal mines takeover was evidently very popular with the mafias, especially of the producing areas. The General Insurance Company (GIC), which was a holding company meant to hold all private insurance players now taken over by Indira's regime, remained in the background.

To add to the rapidly growing public sector was the hospital sector. Anyone who could not run his factory, which employed thousands of workers, just declared a lockout and the government was a ready taker. The sick textile mills were one example but these also included many a prestigious engineering name like Braithwaite which designed and built the first Howrah Bridge which in the 1930s was a wonder. Then there was Jessop & Co, another giant, and the jute mills. The government was looked upon as a saviour. 'See how many jobs Indira is saving', people said.

One way to privatise, and do so transparently is for the President of India to sell all the shares of PSUs to the LIC, GIC, UTI, banks and other financial institutions et al. Payments need not all be made immediately. The better viable units would get picked up by common investors, who would buy 50 to 5,000 shares each. There are many who are hungry for opportunities to invest their savings. This is due to a fall in interest rates. Those units which are unviable will need support either through mergers or through rationalisation, or even through injection of funds. Outright sales are difficult since there are not many entrepreneurs who would have liquid money on the scale required. Moreover, there would always be the likelihood of the Opposition members questioning the sale price, whereas in a public issue of shares, this issue would not arise. It would then be up to the shareholders to elect their board of directors as well as the chief executive and chairman.

The current chief executives of PSUs have to report to the government, which in effect means a Joint Secretary or Additional Secretary. Although well-educated, these officers would be more wedded to procedure than profits. They are unlikely to be *au fait* (acquainted) with the culture of commerce and industry. If some of the public issues (IPOs) of shares do not prove resoundingly popular, the financial institution holding the shares would be left with 40, 50 or 60 percent shares in their possession. So what? In business, it does not matter who owns how many shares—what matters is the quality of management.

Not very long ago, Larsen & Toubro shares were 54 percent owned by the financial institutions. The managing director had about four percent and his friends and relatives had another 12 percent. The rest of the shares were with the public. Yet, the company has the image of a private sector company and runs well.

A concept that requires clarification is that the public sector in no way represents socialism; it is pure state capitalism. The Soviet Union in that sense was a state that practised state capitalism and crashed into bankruptcy. The example of the old Larsen & Toubro was nearer socialism because the shares were with the public, with the management owning only about 16 percent. Uncannily, the large American corporations—many of them—have their managements holding only a small percentage of shares. The rest are held by the public as well as mutual funds.

There is one publicly accepted rule in the USA that if an entrepreneur thinks that he can run a particular company, he can give a public offer to buy all the shares of that company at a higher price than the market. It is for the company directors to decide if they should recommend to the shareholders to hold the shares or sell out. In other words, because of this rule, the managers of these companies are always on their toes, for fear of a takeover bid.

White and Blue Collar Outdated, think of No Collar

LATELY, A NOVEL concept of 'entrepreneurship' has come into currency, whereby a corporation enables and encourages its executives to develop entrepreneurial aptitude. Hopefully, as a result, the company doing so would become aggressively commercial with more profits and greater growth. This is an imaginative concept, but in a country with small to medium corporates, such an imaginative proposal could be fraught with risks.

Such apprehension is not without reason. The first thought that would cross the mind of an ambitious executive would be how he could possibly acquire the business of his employer(s) by displacing the current leading shareholders. If he finds acquisition by this route beyond his reach for the time being, he might get busy trying to get hold of the business secrets of the company, in order to set up a parallel business of his own. All this while, the executive's time and energy would be lost to his employer. If he eventually feels frustrated, he would possibly think of how he could dip his hands in the till.

It is interesting that in the history of British association with India, which clocked over three hundred years till 1947, there were innumerable incidents of its white officials, both of the East India Company and later the Crown, privately accepting presents, big or small, from suppliers as well as clients. The saga can be said to have begun with the man from Shropshire (England), Robert Clive, a writer (the term used then in India for an office clerk) for the East India Company, who is the first dazzling example of this practice. Clive went on to lay the foundation for the military and political supremacy of the Company by ending the saga of Siraj-ud-Daulah, the nawab of Bengal, and the *nawabi* itself and laid his hands on its treasury; in today's terms, the sum that came into Clive's hands would be an estimated £2.325 billion. Clive's rewards included another £30,000 (approximately £11 million in 2020) in return for supporting Mir Jafar—the turncoat who had crossed over in the Battle of Plassey—on the throne. This was in the form of a grant of a *jagir*.

Warren Hastings, who was made the first Governor-General of the East India Company's interests in India, had many Indian friends who plied him with presents. Both these distinguished gentlemen ended up being tried by the British Parliament. Yet, at no stage did it cross either's mind to become the nawab of Bengal or the sultan of Bengal, Bombay and Madras. One ought to recall that in those pre-steamship times, ships with sails would ordinarily take about three months to reach India from England. The alternative was to write letters to dismiss the usurper. That was British loyalty to the Company and the Crown.

In all the years the British traded in India, presents,

whether legitimate or exaggerated, were taken by their officials; but never was an owner replaced by his executive. In contrast, my businesses based in Kolkata, Vadodara and Mumbai were nearly usurped by the very men who were the founder chief executives with my full trust and backing.

In the context of employment, the subject raised is important. On a worldwide basis, only half the people employed have jobs. The other half are self-employed. This includes professionals like doctors, lawyers, chartered accountants and at the other end, hawkers, shopkeepers, porters, etc. The proliferation of economic activity in the liberalisation era has spawned a whole new world of service providers ranging from healthcare, tourism, education, software services and even weddings, which have become full-fledged businesses by themselves.

What is, therefore, of more relevance in such a changing milieu is the establishment of schools that can expose young men and women to the knowhow of starting small businesses, and the dos and don'ts of the same. Yes, there are innumerable institutes of management in the country—another business that has seen huge proliferation—but they normally do not produce future entrepreneurs. Instead, they send out future business managers. The institutions that can produce future business people still seem to be missing. At the elementary level, as far as it is known, there are no schools that guide a young person on how to set up a shop, small or big.

Self-employment is today crucial, more than ever before. More and more women are seeking jobs. More and more young men and women are migrating to the towns and cities from the villages. This is because landholdings have shrunk because of the rising population, and have become too small to accommodate the needs of a normal-sized family. On the other hand, the more sophisticated technology becomes, the lesser would be the number of people employed in establishments.

Yet politicians, especially at election time, never tire of promising "jobs, jobs and more jobs" if elected. From where would they produce these jobs, no one knows. The entire country needs to be exposed to the national problem of unemployment. The days of white collar and blue collar jobs are passing out, while functions that do not have the status of any collar are gaining traction.

Hitler and Xi Jinping

NOT SO LONG ago, General Chi Haotian, a retired general of the People's Liberation Army (PLA) of China said, "Only countries like the United States, Canada and Australia have the vast land to serve our need for mass colonization". Evidently, he forgot to think of Siberia, which is comparably vast and scarcely populated, and more convenient to capture because of its neighbouring location. The general's words "for mass colonization" in the German language would be *lebensraum* or living space. Incidentally, a search for *lebensraum* was Adolf Hitler's excuse for conquering Europe. This was set out in detail by Hitler in his notorious autobiography *Mein Kampf*.

Xi Jinping, China's President for life, does not appear to have written his autobiography, but his will to dominate the world is nevertheless as eloquent as any *Mein Kampf* can be. The question is, many a country is anxious to stop Xi from going ahead with his greed, but how many are willing to actually act? All of Europe knew of the danger Hitler posed, but many wanted "peace in our time" in the words of the then British Prime Minister Neville Chamberlain. This was after he and French Prime Minister Édouard Daladier met Hitler at Munich in 1938, along with Italy's Benito Mussolini. Neither prime minister had a conscience about surrendering to Hitler one of the three regions of what is today the Czech Republic. They endorsed his gobbling up of Sudetenland, leaving behind only Moravia and Bohemia; which also were unilaterally gobbled up by the Nazis within six months. Uncannily, Xinjiang as well as Tibet were grabbed by China with comparable lack of conscience on the morrow of Mao Zedong's successful revolution in 1949, ten years after Hitler's misappropriations. On both occasions, the rest of the world watched with cool indifference. How many more million km does the yellow giant wish to trample upon?

Adolf Hitler came to power in 1933 and committed suicide in 1945 (in all 12 years), whereas Xi Jinping, at age 67, may have a good number of years to go. Fortunately, the US has shown it is not oblivious to the Chinese threat. It has appointed a special coordinator to talk directly to the representative of the Tibetan government-in-exile, a post that had been vacant for long. Robert Destro, the new American special coordinator for Tibet's issues will directly talk to the Tibetan people through its government-in-exile headquartered in Dharamshala, in Himachal Pradesh of India. This is an opportune US initiative which His Holiness the Dalai Lama should respond to with vigour. First, he should be free to publicly tell the young citizens of Tibet to come over to Mcleod Ganj. If they like, he would guarantee their employment, perhaps as his bodyguards and in other echelons of his government-in-exile. He should not be shy of taking American help. The combination of American readiness, India being far better equipped than before, and above all, China having antagonised many a country is a potent one. It would be unfortunate for the people of Tibet if the Dalai Lama does not get into an initiative mode. Opportunity does not materialise every day, which he well knows. Napoleon once defined destiny as "catching luck while it is flying". Above all, he should immediately nominate his successor.

In all probability, the world could have been in a happier situation had President Richard Nixon and his Secretary of State Henry Kissinger not shown haste to go to Beijing to pay their respects to Mao Zedong in 1972. Their reasoning was that the Soviet Iron Curtain was impenetrable whereas the Chinese Bamboo Curtain was easier to enter. So they entered the Red world and opened the gates of the free world to exploit any or every economy; never mind that between Mao's conservatism, Deng Xiao Ping's enterprise and Xi Jinping's aggressiveness, there isn't much difference. It would now appear that the World Trade Organisation (WTO) was promoted unwittingly for the sake of Chinese exports. It is difficult to think of any country that has benefitted over a period by importing Chinese goods. Yes, in the short run, China helped its clients to reduce their costs of production, but given a few years, they became helplessly dependent.

Take for instance an item like the toothbrush. For the nylon bristles, every manufacturer is dependent on the yellow giant. There are manufacturers of the nylon bristles in India, but they too have to depend on China for the import of some of the raw materials. Why were the Chinese costs of production across the board lower than the world's? The new entrepreneur was leased land for practically no rent. To build the factory the banks gave him term loans, often for as low as one percent per annum. He was seldom harassed for neglecting repayment of the loan. So long as he produced hard currency exports to the tune of say, 75 percent of his production, such an exercise amounted to converting the Chinese currency into the dollar.

The smaller entrepreneurs did not have to go out of China to look for markets. Public sector agencies did the finding out as to which country imported what and consumed which products. Most such Chinese manufactures operated their export business with the help of English-speaking Chinese agents. This is the package which enabled the Chinese to supply even Ganesh statuettes at prices lower than that of any other supplier.

With the foreign exchange thus earned and accumulated, China extends loans to smaller countries, whether Sri Lanka, Myanmar, Kenya or other countries of Africa. If any borrower happens not to abide by the terms of repayment, its national assets, given as collateral security, are taken over; for example, Hambantota port, near Galle in Sri Lanka.

Even as this is being written, there are reports of thousands of Chinese citizens fleeing Hong Kong out of fear of the next wave of crackdown by China. The exodus is mainly to the UK. "The Hong Kong we knew no longer exists" is the common refrain.

The Trump administration imposed sanctions against China for what was identified as China's covert war on the US. It can now be said that Covid-19 pandemic, which has devastated the world, has been unleashed on the world by China—it is being termed the Wuhan virus with good reason. Global outrage against China which was initially muted is now becoming more vocal.

For India particularly, China's bellicosity and aggression on the Ladakh border is a reminder that all displays of bonhomie notwithstanding, the yellow neighbour is not going to change its attitude. China views India as a rival to be cut down to size. The fact that India has, under Modi, shed its timidity and is ready to stare the dragon in the eye is even more infuriating. China's support for Pakistan, a known sponsor of jihadi terrorism, has been to keep India on the boil.

Hitler in 1939 spoke of this non-aggression pact and referred to Germany's friendship with Poland as "one of the calming phenomena of European political life". That "calm" could not last even eight months. China under Mao similarly spoke of friendship and amity with India. Its premier Chou En Lai signed the Panchsheel Treaty in 1954, only to stab India in the back in 1962. Earlier in 1959, China invaded Tibet and has been illegally occupying it ever since, not to mention the unrelenting genocide of Tibetans and ceaseless attempts to wipe out Tibet's culture. Its north-eastern province of Xinjiang, home to the Muslim Uygur community who do not see themselves as Chinese, is the target of the communist state's brutal repression and slow genocide, which has intensified after Xi came to power. Any "business-as-usual" approach to China, therefore, is like the appeasement of Hitler in the run up to WWII.

Tragi-Comedy at Delhi

THOSE AGITATORS WHO were holding India's capital to ransom in the name of farmers had asked for a tractor rally on Republic Day. Most governments would have refused as it was a day of our Constitution celebration and perhaps offered a day before or a day after 26 January. To the delight of some agitators and to the surprise of others, the government accepted the idea subject to police discipline. No one, it would seem, suspected the dangers of the tractor *tamasha*, namely the hooligans and the enormity of the damage they could do to the cause. The day witnessed the worst rioting one could have seen or imagined except that not a drop of blood was shed; one death was that of a tractor driver in an accident. For the farmers, the tragedy blew up their two-month cause demonstrated on the chilly highways around Delhi. For the government, it was an unexpected bonanza.

Only the Left Front could enact comedy on the streets of Calcutta (now Kolkata) whenever its ruling government called a protest *bandh* against whom no one knew, although it was impeccably enforced. Not a bird flew near any of the many streets of the city. The press was free to move. The boys at street corners guarding the *bandh* were often keen to be interviewed and photographed.

It was a comedy for all those citizens who enjoyed a holiday but a tragi-comedy for the poor in the unorganised sector. The rickshawalas, taxi drivers, bus operators, the *mutias* or coolies et al had to go without wages. When I asked a boy at a street corner his reply was that these men do not belong to our unions; so what do we owe them? Working class was an expression too distant for the boy.

The most tragic rioting that Calcutta has ever witnessed was between 16 and 18 August 1946. It was an attempt by MA Jinnah to convince London that Hindus and Muslims could not coexist; hence Partition. I quote briefly from the official letter of the Governor of Bengal to the Secretary of State:

> The scale of rioting was unprecedented. It was a pogrom between two rival armies of the Calcutta underworld. The fact that over 2,000 persons of the "goonda" type who had been confined under the Defence of India Rules during the war were released the previous year is of great significance.
>
> The only thing which prevented a complete collapse of the administration was the three battalions of British troops, who were readily available for this sort of emergency. Though the occasion and nature of the emergency could not be foreseen, the Army Commander and I had long agreed on the necessity of such a disposition of troops. I could not possibly have held Calcutta with the police alone, and I am doubtful if the Indian troops would have inspired sufficient confidence.

> That the infection did not spread immediately to the districts is a fact for which we cannot be too thankful. We had to take a big chance in denuding Howrah and the mill areas of troops on the 17th.
>
> The obligations of the Constitution made my task far harder. My special responsibility for law and order is not a "discretionary" matter, and in handling the situation, particularly at the outset, I had always to consider the susceptibilities of my Ministry. The dual personality of Suhrawardy as Chief Minister (in charge of the Home portfolio) and as the most influential member of the Muslim League in Bengal, was a constant embarrassment.
>
> Yours sincerely,
>
> FJ Burrows

CC: Lord Wavell, Viceroy

What was an even more tragic event, although bloodless, was the partition of Bengal in 1905. The idea was not new; it was bubbling since 1875. By dividing Bengal on communal lines and encouraging Muslim ascendancy in the east, the government was, in the words of British colonial administrator Risley, weakening "a solid body of opponents" to the Raj. Viceroy Curzon was presented with hundreds of petitions which he chose to ignore. Bengal united was a power; Bengal divided would pull in several different directions. The summer of 1905 was a long, hot one in Bengal and the atmosphere was charged with tension. The editor of a leading daily had condemned Partition. Overnight, emotions had risen to a fever pitch. People refused to participate in festivities where foreign salt or sugar was used. The giant was stirring and even the Viceroy was forced to admit that "the spectacle that has been presented by the streets of Calcutta during the past fortnight has not in my opinion been creditable to the Capital of a great Empire".

August 16, the day of the tragedy, became a turning point in British India's history. The announcement of Partition shattered the long, legendary belief in the eventual fairness of the British. It became a day of national mourning. No food was cooked in Calcutta homes, the domestic hearths remained unlit. Shops and offices were closed and in several places newspapers were not distributed. Poet Rabindranath's song '*Banglar mati Banglar jal*' thrilled patriotic sentiments to an all-time high and the ball had been set rolling for the mass *Raksha Bandhan* ceremony. Virtual strangers stopped each other on the streets to tie the *rakhi* thread, symbolising brotherhood.

A Green Star over Bengal

ASADUDDIN OWAISI IS a politician with blue blood, with a surname imported from Arabia, and a leadership of a century-old party founded by Nawab Mahmood Nawaz Khan. In 1944, Razakar leader Qasim Rizvi was selected as the party's leader, to also become the extra-militia force of the Nizam of Hyderabad.

In 1957, Qasim Rizvi was exiled to Pakistan but before departing, he handed over the Majlis-e-Ittehadul-Muslimeen (MIM) to his right-hand man Abdul Wahid Owaisi. His son Sultan Salahuddin took over the party in 1975; it was then inherited by his illustrious son Asaduddin. The party headquarters are based in an impressive building called Darus Salam near Hyderabad's famed Charminar.

Asaduddin Owaisi inherited a single Lok Sabha seat, the Hyderabad city constituency. If the MIM is today an all-India name, the credit must go to him. Soon after the television channel CNN-IBN was established, by a stroke of coincidence he was fielded against me in a half an hour programme with Sagarika Ghosh as the anchor. Our debate was on a sensitive communal controversy. The anchor asked for his comments first, to which I reacted that Mr Owaisi's views might be coloured by those prevailing in a neighbouring country. His counter-reaction was explosive. Asaduddin threatened to bite off some assembly seats in Bengal

West Bengal's explosive electioneering this time around did not see much of the Owaisi rhetoric in action, possibly because this smart Muslim politician did not wish to split his community's votes and thereby end up helping the incumbent chief minister. Mamata Banerjee might have escaped being singed by his political campaigning this time around, but Owaisi is not one to sit quietly. What Mamta and other provincial politicians fail to gauge is that for Muslim voters, there are no 'insiders' or 'outsiders'. The issue of language (a sensitive point in Bengal though other states in India have left this particular kind of sentimentality behind), other than Urdu, is of no importance. It is the sacred thread of Islam that binds them all. Muslims are *momins* (believers); the others, however neighbourly, are 'different' or the 'other'. Hindu arguments do not cut ice with the Muslims.

I reckon that the Hyderabadi politician's appeal to his flock in the forthcoming assembly as well as the general elections would be to mobilise and vote for him and his party, because he will do everything for them. Owaisi would have absolutely no qualms in declaring that he has no loyalty other than towards the faithful of Allah the Merciful, whereas those opposition parties professing to be secular also have other communities to cater to. His party the MIM would be exclusively for the *ummah* (the community of Muslims) while the other opposition parties would have to divide their commitments between various segments of the majority Hindu population as well. In other words, they cannot exclusively cater to Muslim interests alone, which he can, unfettered.

The result of this secular duality has been the *Tareekh-e-Intekhab*, or the history of elections in India. That means the so-called Indian political version of secularism; flatter the Muslim, occasionally frighten him with a riot and then protect him, then go back to flattery. In the eyes of Allah the Merciful, he may be a *momin*, but in the view of the vote harvester, he is a tiger in the cage of a circus; the only grouse being that he is so ill-fed that he cannot attack. Jawaharlal Nehru once said that he was a Hindu only by accident; he was a Muslim by culture and an Englishman by upbringing. He, therefore, knew how to make a Muslim tick, which he had to for the Congress in the immediate years after Independence was dominated by those loyal to Sardar Patel. Nehru had to build his own support base. Muslims, traumatised by Partition, were his obvious first choice. Reportedly, they voted nearly 90 percent whereas in the early elections, the rest of the voters polled not much more than 45 percent. The net result was that one Muslim voter was worth two Hindus.

Things have changed with the march of time. More Hindus go to the polling booths today. The late Muslim politician Syed Shahabuddin once wrote in a national daily that if there were a choice between development and identity for his community, it would opt for identity. In Nehru's days, by electing him, the Muslim love for identity won. Although they were poor, India was a wonderful country. Lately, Hindu candidates are winning more because their community votes more. India in the perception of many Muslims, therefore, has become an 'insecure' country.

For all these reasons, the Muslim clusters wherever they be, are in search of new heroes; the parties of the old ones appear to be folding up. One such superhero is Asaduddin. What can parties opposed to the BJP and competing for the Muslim vote do to counter this powerful appeal? One likely counter, hackneyed as it would be, would be that Muslims alone cannot form a government; they are too few to do so. They have to combine with others and only then can they win the support of a sympathetic majority. Here, one might go back to the days of the late Babu Jagjivan Ram, who ended up as the Deputy Prime Minister of India. Never in his political career did he publicly discuss his caste. Had he done so, he might have won a maximum of 18 percent votes. From where would he have gathered a minimum of another 36 percent? The same will be the problem with Owaisi. Can he form a government in any state? 'Secular' parties would therefore harangue the Muslims and ask them why they should waste their votes on such a party. It is undeniable though that the *ummah* has given some votes in Bihar to Owaisi and elected five MLAs. It remains to be seen what the MIM can do in Uttar Pradesh and the next general elections.

After one or two elections, in the event of climbing on to some ascendancy, we would have to watch whether Owaisi and his party could pose a threat to the integrity of the country. After all, we should not forget the Partition of 1947. Soon after August 1947, HS Suhrawardy, the former Premier of undivided Bengal wrote to Chaudhry Khaliquzzaman in UP that the strategy for the Muslims left behind in India should be to gather in clusters or mega ghettos. Not to be glossed over is the fact that Khaliquzzaman became the President of the Muslim League in Pakistan after Jinnah passed away. This advice might imply that if several clusters gathered together in due course, more partitions could be engineered. The government of India should watch out for and discourage such cluster formations from now on.

The one consolation we have is that Owaisi hails from a land of dreamers, like Nizam Mir Osman Ali. He had Ali Yavar Jung, then Secretary Constitutional Affairs to present the rather fantastic view that the Portuguese colonial regime considered Marmagoa to be a dead weight and would be willing to sell it at a reasonable price. The idea of buying Goa was too attractive to be dissipated by a heavy dose of realism. When World War II had ended, the prospects of success seemed brighter. On Hyderabad's side the prime mover was Sir Mirza Ismail (the Diwan of Mysore, Jaipur and Hyderabad) with Sir Walter Monckton (a British politician) as a close second.

The parleys in Lisbon had become known in India. Once India became independent, it was unlikely to acquiesce for long to Portugal's rule over Goa, just as it rejected Hyderabad's claim to independence. Still less would it permit Hyderabad's transit rights over land or air space to connect it to other parts of India. If only Hyderabad could possess a port like Marmagoa, it would add enormously to its political importance, and would ensure its economic development in a most satisfactory manner.

A meeting between the Portuguese and Hyderabad negotiators was arranged on 1 November 1947. It was attended by the Portuguese Prime Minister Salazar, Sir Alexander Roger and Antonio Bastroff Silva. In bitter retrospect, the devoted Hyderabadi writer Zubeida Yazdani made two points. One was about Mir Osman Ali Khan's 'megalomaniac notions' which caused him 'to lose the balance of his mind'. Her other grievance was that 'the Nizam depended too strongly on the Muslim League for the achievement of his goal, which was an independent Muslim state in the south of India'. Those dreams soon turned to dust.

West Bengal and Bangladesh

AS LUCIDLY BROUGHT out by Prof Timur Koran, a Turkish American who teaches at Duke University USA, the practice of Islam inhibits business growth and, therefore, does not enable economic progress or development. The prohibition of usury is an example. This explains why Islamic societies have not been economically productive. Therefore, they had to become adept at the conquest of other lands in search of resources.

Bangladesh has an added handicap. For centuries, the Bengali elite were land-owning rather than businessmen. The Bangladeshi culture took its cue from the Bengali elite. Islam is a comprehensive prescription for living, including politics. The Quran is the ultimate reference point. No Muslim ruler can deviate from that path. Ideally, *jamhuriyat* or consensus is the solution. Monarchy, autocracy or oligarchy are the only alternatives, which leaves democracy no space.

Sheikh Hasina, the current prime minister has won two terms, is relatively secular and grateful to India for the freedom of Bangladesh. Her predecessor, Begum Khaleda Zia, was not. Khaleda's husband Zia-ur-Rahman was almost pro-Pakistani, being a Muslim ashraf. But what after Hasina retires or relinquishes power? Would not there be a change in the country's foreign policy, especially vis-à-vis India?

It is uncanny that it was the Bengali-Hindu elite which founded a Hindu political ideology. Raj Narayan Bose is reputed to have coined the term 'Hindutva', or at least used it for the first time in the year 1863. He was the maternal grandfather of Yogi Aurobindo Ghosh. The Hindu Anushilan Samiti was founded and functioned only in Bengal, with the great poet Rabindranath Tagore being its leading light. The movement against the partition of Bengal in 1905 was largely led by Yogi Aurobindo, and was actively supported by Tagore. The Bengal Renaissance was a Hindu phenomenon.

The withdrawal of the partition of Bengal by Emperor George V in 1911 at the Delhi Durbar was the inauguration of so-called secularism in Bengal. The Bengali elite began regretting their conduct towards Muslims. For example, inviting a Muslim co-villager to a wedding dinner, making him sit separately to eat and then expecting him to carry his own thali to clean. This is only one example.

With the rise of Netaji Subhas Bose, the Hindu-Muslim cordiality tended towards friendship. The moderate leader Fazlur Rahman of the Krishak Party became the Premier of Bengal and this secular trend continued. By early 1947, Netaji's elder brother Sarat Bose, Fazlur Rahman and Sir Abdul Rahim (a leading member of the Muslim League) were discussing the prospects of a third dominion, namely, undivided Bengal in addition to India and Pakistan.

After Independence, the Nehruvian ethos and the appeasement of Muslims for their votes inflated this trend. Partition, which displaced many Hindus, did not lead to any real antagonism against the Muslims in Bengal in its immediate aftermath as well as later, so much so that being associated with the RSS, the Hindu Mahasabha or the Jana Sangh became infra dig. The Hindu political movement could not throw up a popular leader after Dr Syama Prasad Mookerjee died mysteriously in Kashmir. The Jana Sangh leader Prof Haripada Bharati was respected but had no mass appeal. The secular show persisted and infiltrators from Bangladesh were encouraged for their votes.

The Islamist penny dropped at last in the Bengali-Hindu mind. There was a cataclysmic change in the thinking of people in West Bengal before the approaching assembly elections. For decades, West Bengal had resisted the domination of what the *bhadralok* elite of the state would call a "Hindi heartland party" and had prided itself on its avowedly secular outlook; the Bengali identity has been preponderant over the religious one.

However, the incessant mollycoddling of the religious minority slowly but surely brought an about-turn in the Bengali mind, to the extent that even the most secular among them had begun to fear that their State might become another Bangladesh. The first major sign of West Bengal's changing political mood was the 2019 Lok Sabha election in which the BJP won 18 out of 42 parliamentary seats.

West Bengal is in the news very much these days with ruling Trinamool Congress and the incumbent Chief Minister Mamata Banerjee having pulled off another assembly election victory by winning 221 seats while BJP won only 77.

Bengali and 'Outsider'

IN REPLYING TO Mamata Banerjee's allegation that the Bharatiya Janata Party is an "outsider" organisation, while she herself is the "daughter of Bengal", the prime minister, at the Brigade Ground speech on 7 March 2021, remarked that Trinamool had been spawned by the Congress. The Indian National Congress was founded in 1885 by a retired bureaucrat, Allan Octavian Hume, an Englishman. The communist parties of India were all spawns of the Communist Party of the Soviet Union. Their ideology was authored entirely by Karl Marx. Vladimir Lenin brought the Bolshevik Party to power with the revolution of 1917. A premier street in Calcutta celebrated Lenin's coming to power by being named "Lenin Sarani". It is opposite the Metro cinema, near the Dharamtolla Street. Incidentally, the old Harrington Street where the US Consulate is situated was renamed by Chief Minister Jyoti Basu as Ho Chi Minh Sarani.

I once took a client visiting from Germany around the city for half a day. He found every CPM graffiti to be a sketch of the Soviet dictator Josef Stalin and wondered—why Stalin now? Is there no Indian leader attractive enough to catch votes? In the Second World War, Stalin wanted to arouse Russians to fight for their motherland, in complete contrast to Leon Trotsky's earlier call for a "permanent revolution" and Karl Marx's *Communist Manifesto,* which called upon the workers of the world to unite.

Mamata Banerjee has never once termed these things foreign or from outside. She finds Hindutva and its slogan Jai Shri Ram "outsiders", despite the fact that it was Raj Narayan Bose, the grandfather of Yogi Aurobindo Ghosh who had coined the term Hindutva for the first time in 1863. Leading Bengalis, including Gurudev Rabindranath Tagore, were members of the aggressively Hindu Anushilan Samiti. The Samiti had become particularly active after the first partition of Bengal in 1905, until 1911, when the partition was withdrawn by King George V.

Hindu ideology is not anti-anyone. The word Hindu has been the identity for the entire subcontinent. In 1930, my father's professor at the University of Boston asked him what he was. The reply was: "I am an Indian". The professor replied, "We have plenty of Indians in America. You are probably a Hindu. My question is—are you a Hindu Christian, a Hindu Muslim or a Hindu Hindu?" In other words, for the world outside, Hindu and Hinduism are the markers of India's identity.

Coming to the "Bengali versus outsider" debate, it bears iteration here that it was a prominent Bengali, born 120 years ago, who founded a nationalist party that dominates Indian politics today. This is none other than Dr Syama Prasad

Mookerjee, a towering intellectual, academician and political leader. The party he founded, the Bharatiya Jana Sangh, was the only true opposition to the then hegemonic ruling Congress. Its later avatar became the Bharatiya Janata Party (BJP) which not only rules India and has become the world's biggest political party, but has also decimated the once mighty Congress.

One must not forget that it was Dr Mookerjee who salvaged West Bengal and led the Hindus of the erstwhile undivided Bengal to grab a slice of their homeland from the nefarious designs of Muhammad Ali Jinnah and his Muslim League, by effectively resisting the blatantly-biased Muslim League provincial government of Bengal.

Bengal's Hindus were the second-largest ethnic minority after the Muslims in undivided Bengal (nearly 42 percent). But they were subjected to two horrific rounds of genocide, first in Calcutta in August 1946, following Jinnah's clarion call for 'Direct Action' (the Great Calcutta Killing) and then in Noakhali and Tippera districts of eastern Bengal in October that year. Nearly 10,000 Hindus were massacred and thousands of Hindu women were raped in this orgy of violence orchestrated by Bengal Premier HS Suhrawardy himself. Dr Mookerjee, the indisputable leader of Bengal's Hindus, recognised the looming threat as early as 1940 when he had said in Sylhet (then in Assam): "The dangers in front of us are many; the latest addition in the shape of a movement for Pakistan should not be brushed aside lightly. Jinnah is out to destroy the very soul of India". The looming danger was the pernicious dream of a so-called 'United Bengal', promoted by Suhrawardy, Nazimuddin (one of the founding fathers of Pakistan) and Fazlur Rahman (Bengal's revenue minister), supported by Sarat Chandra Bose of the Socialist Republic Party. This 'United Bengal' movement, a smokescreen to grab all of Bengal for Pakistan, had Jinnah's blessings. Had this League plan materialised, the Hindus of Bengal would have suffered a plight similar to that of Sindh's Hindus who have been left without a country to call their own.

The incorporation of all of these into Pakistan was foiled only by the concerted and unanimous efforts of Bengal's Hindus led resolutely by Dr Syama Prasad Mookerjee, who formed the Bengal Partition League towards the end of 1946 to demand a separate Hindu-Bengali homeland. He obtained the support of all sections of Bengali society, from the *bhadralok* to the rural pleasantry. League sections of communists and socialists too had to support the partition of Bengal—the Muslim League didn't spare Hindu communists.

The supreme irony is that Mamata might not have had even an identity, leave alone a state, but for the heroic efforts of Dr Syama Prasad Mookerjee, whose party she now dubs an "outsider".

Bengal and Change

THERE IS NO getting away from the fact that without the full benefit of Bengal and its intelligent people, India has been functioning without a part of its intellect. From the lofty pedestal of scientists, administrators and managers down to the factory worker, the state's people are clever and skillful. Today, they are being wasted for lack of opportunities, which were destroyed as the state fell from being India's industrial jewel to the lamentable state of the graveyard of industry. I believe that a Bengali can operate the domain of information technology with as much ease and skill, as say people in the southern Indian states. But where is the environment that would give such opportunities to the young men and women of Kolkata?

West Bengal could also be the education hub for the region stretching from UP in the west to Assam in the east, including Bihar, Nepal and Bangladesh. Bengalis still value learning and at their best, are excellent teachers. A school or college/university would cost approximately no more than

Rs 25 crores each. Similarly, professional management should be used to tone up all hospitals with two objectives in mind—one, to enable medical colleges to be developed at the side and secondly, wherever possible, help attracting medical tourism. This again would need incurring expenses to the tune of Rs 25 crores per establishment or perhaps a little more. The World Bank can provide the finance so long as the state government can give guarantees.

The setting up of heavier industries would entail problems. For instance, units would have long gestation periods having to compete with the rest of the world, apart from needing thousands of crores of rupees in investment. The Himalayas are God's gift to north Bengal, with greater potential for tourism than even Switzerland. What, however, is required is an infrastructure for attracting tourists. There is space for laying out an international airport in Bagdogra. What probably is necessary is to invite a couple of international airlines and hotel chains and provide them some undertakings and help for the initial stages, whereby they can deliver the rest. Not everyone knows that from Sandakphu at 12,000 feet—not far from Darjeeling—one can view Mount Everest all day, given a clear sky. Kanchenjunga and several other mountain ranges are visible from Darjeeling, a hill station town that is in need of a qualitative upgrade. The employment potential of such development would also be considerable.

It does not matter which party or ideology brings these changes in its train, so long as it delivers the goods. After Independence, West Bengal was ruled by Nehruvian socialism. Thereafter, the United Front, a hotchpotch of parties and then the Left Front led by the Communist Party of India (Marxist), i.e., the CPM (which meant Marxist rule), came to power. These were foreign ideologies, which did not help economic development. We have now had ten years of the Trinamool Congress (TMC), with a daughter of Bengal as its leader.

Strangely, Mamata Banerjee calls the BJP an "outsider". Being comparatively young, she may not be aware that the BJP's previous avatar the Bharatiya Jana Sangh (BJS) was conceived on Cornwallis Street in Kolkata. There, Guru Golwalkar, head of the Rashtriya Swayamsevak Sangh (RSS) had a meeting with Dr Syama Prasad Mookerjee of the Hindu Mahasabha, whose resolute leadership had prevented all of Bengal becoming Pakistan and saved West Bengal for Hindus. At this Cornwallis Street meeting, it was decided to form a political arm of the indigenous political ideology of Hindutva. Dr Mookerjee would lead this political arm, and to help him in this task, the RSS would provide him two stalwarts per province. The political ideology of Hindutva is about the only one that has risen from the soil of Asia. All the 'isms'—whether capitalism, socialism, communism or fascism, were born and bred in Europe.

If, therefore, anyone is an outsider, it is these ideologies. The term 'Hindutva' was first pronounced in 1863 by Raj Narayan Bose, the maternal grandfather of Sri Aurobindo. The aggressive Hindu Anushilan Samiti was led by Sri Aurobindo when the 1905 partition of Bengal took place. Gurudev Rabindranath Tagore was a leading light of the Samiti, which organised the agitation against this partition so effectively that Emperor George V annulled it in 1911. Thereafter, Bengal's leaders began taking a sympathetic view of the Muslims for having lost their new province of East Bengal and Assam. In the bargain, the Muslims were treated more gently. Being Bengali became more important than being Hindu.

Nevertheless, during the era of the freedom movement, Bengal sent out tall national leaders like Deshbandhu Chittaranjan Das and the redoubtable Netaji Subhas Chandra Bose. Bengali leaders did not confine themselves to the eastern corner of India but played on the all-India field. Given a well-governed state, these glories can be revived again. Incidentally, Bengal has contributed in no small way to the growth of Hindi. Apart from being the pioneer of a number of Bengali newspapers, the great scholar and reformist leader Raja Ram Mohan Roy also encouraged journalism in Hindi, leading to the publication of Hindi journals like *Samvad Chandrika*. Roy also wrote Hindi in the Devanagari script. In fact, the saga of Hindi journalism begins from Bengal with the first-ever Hindi newspaper *Udant Martand* published in Calcutta in 1826. Sarat Chandra Chattopadhyay, the highly popular Bengali novelist of the early 20th century is as widely read outside Bengal as he is in his home state. In fact, Sarat Chandra remains the most popular, translated and adapted Indian writer of all time.

And how can one forget Bankim Chandra Chatterjee and his magnum opus *Ananda Math* with its invocation to the Mother Divine, the soul-stirring "Vande Mataram?" Vande Mataram not only became the inspirational fountainhead for Indian patriots during the independence movement, but in later decades also became the war cry for Hindu nationalism, which burst forth with renewed vigour with the launch of the Ram Janmabhoomi movement in the 1980s. Ironically, Vande Mataram, and also the politico-religious opposition to it, became a fulcrum of the growing sentiment of nationalism. It is highly likely that a *bhadralok*-promoted Bengali exceptionalism grew in direct proportion to the decline of West Bengal, but such exceptionalism never became a mass phenomenon, not even in the heyday of 'progressive' Left rule. West Bengal's identity remains rooted in religiosity.

The electoral tussle of 2021, however, apart from its headline-grabbing daily heat and thunder, also indicates that a yearning, albeit a silent one, to be more integrally a part of the national mainstream is coming into play. This is as it should be for a state that provided the paradigm for modern Indian nationalism. Bengal, after so many decades, now seems to be saying that it is changing, and also very much wants to be a significant part of an India that is changing in a rapid way. Even as we shall be furiously debating and dissecting every aspect of the outcome of the assembly elections in the state, the dictum of China's late leader Deng Xiao Ping, "The colour of the cat does not matter, so long as it catches mice" should be borne in mind. West Bengal has carried the yoke of ideology without deliverance for far too long.

The East India Company and Bengal

AS ELECTIONEERING HAS concluded, many in West Bengal might have recalled how the medieval nawab rule was ended. Bengal's nawab Alivardi Khan died in 1756, succeeded by his impulsive grandson Siraj-ud-Daulah, who ruled from Murshidabad. Siraj, aware of the East India Company's colonising desires and resenting its political, commercial and military presence in Bengal, was also angered by the Company's alleged involvement with some of his court members in a conspiracy to oust him. The Company fortified Fort William and abused trade privileges granted to them by the Mughals. Siraj invaded and captured Calcutta in 1756. His soldiers allegedly locked up some Englishmen in a dungeon in Fort William called the Black Hole, then situated where today's imposing General Post Office stands. Many of them died there.

The East India Company was incensed at Siraj's action and ordered Robert Clive and Admiral Watson to reach Calcutta and teach him a lesson. The Nawab then had an army of a hundred thousand men, but popular discontent against him was brewing. Bengal's merchant princes the Seths, prominent among whom were Madhab Rai (of the Jagat Seth family) and Raja Naba Krishna Deb—whose palace still dominates Sova Bazar in Kolkata—lived in perpetual fear of their wealth under Siraj's despotic rule. They saw this as the opportunity to end his rule. These wealthy men themselves were powerless to remove him so made common cause with the East India Company.

The Nawab's general Mir Jafar wanted to be nawab; his co-conspirators against Siraj-ud-Daulah were Rai Durlabh, Yar Lutuf Khan, Amin Chand and several officers in the army. After Clive and Watson reached Calcutta from Madras by boat, these gentlemen conspired with the English. It was secretly agreed that Jafar with 50,000 sepoys under his command would stand still in the clash between Clive and Siraj. The two armies met on 23 June 1757 at Palashi—hence the name Battle of Plassey—a village not far from Murshidabad on the highway from Kolkata to Siliguri.

Clive had 3,500 soldiers, among them 600 Europeans and the rest Indian sepoys. Siraj's army was arraigned under Mohanlal, his most-trusted commander although Mir Jafar was much senior. Clive's forces waited in an area surrounded by a mango grove while Siraj's army was camped nearby. Its larger battery of artillery began firing to frighten the Company's troops. Mir Jafar did not move, saying he would make the final charge to overwhelm the English and waited. Rumours spread that Jafar was a doubtful starter and Siraj's troops became nervous at this. His ammunition had been rendered wet and practically useless because of a heavy thunderstorm soon after the battle began, whereas the British had covered theirs with tarpaulin. Nervousness soon led to panic.

Siraj-ud-Daulah realised this and retreated to Murshidabad. The inevitable rout of his army had set in and Robert Clive had won. The Nawab collected all his moveable wealth and fled to Rajmahal in Bihar (Bengal then included Bihar and Orissa). It was also the richest *subah* (province) of the Mughal Empire. Until 1707 when Aurangzeb died it was the only province to remit money regularly, which no other *subah* did.

The luckless Siraj was apprehended, brought back to Murshidabad and murdered on the orders of Mir Miran, Mir Jafar's nephew, as part of the agreement between Jafar and the East India Company. There was no visible protest at his downfall and the Englishmen, who were few in numbers, were able to move about in the erstwhile nawabi capital. Does this not indicate that Siraj's rule was not popular? No one was able to foresee the significance of the Battle of Plassey. In 1757, it was seen only as a victory of the Company.

But Plassey was the beginning of the advent of British rule in India and the dethronement of nawabs. On the heels of Plassey, the Battle of Buxar was fought in Bihar in 1764. The Mughals and Mir Qasim, Bengal's new disgruntled nawab were defeated by the Company. Mughal Emperor Shah Alam-II had to surrender the Diwani rights of Bengal, Bihar and Awadh to the Company. The Company then on was authorised to collect taxes from all of Bengal and keep them.

Thereafter, the Company expanded its control over India. In 1799, Governor-General Wellesley eliminated Tipu Sultan of Mysore. Wellesley employed the Subsidiary Alliance, offering protection to Indian kingdoms at their ruler's cost. On failure of payment the ruler would lose his territory to the

Company. By the 1840s, the East India Company extended its sway over much of the subcontinent. Under Governor-General Dalhousie's Doctrine of Lapse, if a ruler did not have a legitimate heir, the Company could grab his kingdom. A ruler accused of misrule, like Awadh's Wajid Ali Shah, could lose his state at the Governor-General's discretion. This eventually provoked the Sepoy Mutiny of 1857-58. After it was put down, the British Crown under Queen Victoria took over India from the East India Company, whose rule was extinguished by the Queen's 1858 proclamation. British rule lasted until 1947, for the next 90 years.

Gopal Krishna Gokhale, a distinguished Congress leader, once said, "What Bengal thinks today, India will think tomorrow". As time unfolded in those early years, he might have said "What Bengal did in 1757, India continued for the next 190 years".

Economy of West Bengal Lagging

UPON INDEPENDENCE, WEST Bengal was one of the most industrialised states in India. British entrepreneurs had invested a great deal in a variety of enterprises ranging from jute mills, coal mines, engineering, tea gardens et al. Paradoxically, it was under British rule that the well-known Industrial Disputes Act was passed at the time the government in Britain was that of the Labour Party. The trade unions in the country and particularly in West Bengal happened to be communist dominated. Between the law, the unions and their conduct, it was not always easy to work. The management had very little expertise in industrial law because the Industrial Disputes Act came into being as late as 1947. West Bengal had to endure many different instances of labour violence. The worst incident was when in one company's factory, two British foremen were thrown into the furnace as a gruesome fallout of a labour protest. There were also several other incidents in various industrial plants.

Coming to another point—due to the national movement as well as the Second World War, very little investment had been made in the industries in India, Bengal being no exception. By end of the war it was time for most of the industries to refurbish and modernise. At that time, with a new India in an uncertain state, the British owners were reluctant to put in fresh money. They, therefore, began to sell their companies whenever an Indian buyer offered a reasonable price. They found that there was no dearth of buyers, because a fair number of Indian businessmen had plentiful profits from the Second World War. Very few of them had knowledge or experience of industry. What the British offered were going concerns. Regrettably, not a single one of these British relinquishments was picked up by ethnic Bengalis. In other words, there were quite a few Indian buyers of these British firms, but none from the soil of West Bengal.

The growing of jute as an alternative to rice was encouraged by the mills; this led to agricultural advancement. The jute-growing areas until then were in East Bengal. Otherwise, farming was left alone in those early years. The idea of three crops a year did not really exist. After the kharif crops were harvested, most farms appeared barren.

But skewed agriculture and stalled progress in industry weren't West Bengal's only problems. Partition had hit the state in a big way, with more than three-fourths of its territory going to East Pakistan (now Bangladesh). Oppressed people from East Pakistan flowed into West Bengal. Large numbers of these people had only farming skills, but there were no farms to give them occupation. At a rough guess, about one-third of the state's population is from the East.

The deterioration of the state's economy could be seen in

Calcutta (Kolkata). Few of today's generation would believe that the city's iconic Park Street, until 1950, looked almost like a street in London. Thereafter, Park Street was relegated to only a place of nostalgia. Incidentally, unlike the Punjab, Bengal saw mostly a one-way traffic in Partition; only a few families migrated to East Pakistan. Over a period of time, illegal infiltration from the East to the West was a perennial complaint since the late 1960s. The population of the state grew but the growth in West Bengal's population was not accompanied by a commensurate growth of economic development. On the contrary, from an advanced industrial state it became a graveyard of industries.

West Bengal's economy now depends on three crops a year and general trading. A historical reason for the state's economy being slow to grow is its people's indifference to business and industry. In 1793, Lord Cornwallis introduced his famous Permanent Settlement whereby zamindars would collect the revenue. Sub-zamindaris were permissible; as a result, a large number of rich families came into being, especially as prices of produce rose, and with them, the earnings. Even if they earned more, they had to pay to the government the same as in 1793.

The much written about Bengal renaissance was attributed to this class. Not surprisingly, there grew a distaste for business and industry, which by its very nature demands strenuous work, enterprise and a willingness and capacity to embrace risk. Thus, sizeable business opportunities slipped through Bengali hands, which in turn, slowed down the economy of West Bengal. In contrast, Gujarat has prospered but there is no great secret to it. The baniyas, the business community are only about 6 percent of the population. But almost every community of the state is keen to get into business, including the adivasis who form 16 percent of the state's population. It is not difficult to explain a simple business proposition in a Gujarat village. Not everyone enjoys music; in contrast, every Bengali enjoys music, but very few among them like business.

After Bidhan Roy who served as Chief Minister of West Bengal from 1948 until his death in 1962, Bengal has not had a CM who can be called economy-savvy.

West Bengal Election

THE RESULTS OF the hard-fought election have been more or less as expected. No doubt Delhi optimists are disappointed because they had hoped for a BJP majority. But their wishes were more like dreams. Understanding Bengal, I concede, is difficult. In an earlier article I have hinted at the unique features of Bengal. In early 1947, Netaji Subhas' elder brother Sarat Bose and Kiran Sarkar on the Hindu side and Sir Abdul Rahim and Fazlur Rahman were negotiating for a united Bengal. This would have been a third independent dominion besides India and Pakistan.

Surprisingly, these friendly negotiations began within a few months of the Great Calcutta Killing of August 1946. Thousands had been killed in the name of Muslim League's Direct Action Day. The instruction to resort to this action came from Jinnah, to convey to the British government that Hindus and Muslims could not coexist in one country and, therefore, Partition had to precede Independence. As a result,

Jinnah insisted on Pakistan being freed on 14th August, one day before India got her Independence.

Jinnah encouraged the two Muslim leaders to somehow achieve a separate united Bengal. The Communist Party also supported Sarat Babu to clinch the deal. The reason was that with its majority Muslim population and a prime minister of the same community, a united Bengal was likely to support Pakistan in preference to India. Earlier, Jinnah had asked Muhammad Saadulla, Premier of Assam from 1939, to categorise the Adivasis as animists and not Hindus. The latter would then become a minority and the Muslims a majority, at least marginally. The idea was to grab Assam for Pakistan. Gopinath Bardoloi saved Assam in the nick of time by rushing to Delhi and getting the Congress high command to intervene.

Incidentally, the national anthems of both India and Bangladesh have been written by Gurudev Tagore. Nazrul Islam was a poet regarded as second only to Tagore. The traditional highway out of the Kolkata Dum Dum airport was named Nazrul Islam Avenue. Today's best Rabindra music singer is a Dhaka lady named Rezwana Choudhury. She usually wears a sari and a red *tika* on her forehead although without *sindoor*. Bangladesh's quarrel with the Pakistani western wing began in February 1948 when Jinnah declared Urdu as Pakistan's only national language. Love for the Bengali language was demonstrated virtually the next day by Dhaka University's students, who rioted on the streets of the city for several days.

From then on to the end of 1971 was a very unhappy time for the East Pakistanis who later became Bangladeshis. They are Bengali first, Bangladeshis second and Muslims third. The majority of the people of West Bengal, more or less, share this order of priority. The BJP, therefore, should consider their 77 seats in the recent elections as a great success and by no means a defeat.

One should not forget that the BJP could hardly field a Bengali-speaking public figure who could address big meetings across West Bengal. This matters a great deal to the Bengali. When I open my mouth and utter a few sentences in Bengali, the listener is surprised and delighted and exclaims: how good your Bengali is! Not because my grasp of the language is very good but because, having been brought up in Kolkata, I know that Bengali is first a melody and then a language. Many third-generation settlers do not realise this and the Bengali listener does not like his language being spoken without its lilt. In Gujarat if any settler speaks in Gujarati, the reaction often is—why has he wasted his energy learning the language? We understand Hindi. That is the infinite love in Bengal for its language.

Anyway, that apart, after Dr Syama Prasad Mookerjee passed away in 1953, for two general elections perhaps four Hindu Mahasabha candidates won MLA seats in Bankura district. Thereafter, the score was zero for every Hindu party. Prof Haripada Bharati was a respected person but he could not become an MLA despite being the leader of Jana Sangh for years and also becoming its national president for a term. One-third approximately of West Bengal is successors of refugees from East Pakistan and Bangladesh. But until 2011, they were supporters of the Left Front. It is strange but true! The Communists had openly supported Partition and yet these people whose families had to flee as refugees did not care.

Given these difficulties, the BJP has done well going from three to seventy-seven seats in a mere five years. The TMC did very well. The parties that were wiped out were the Congress (1) and the Left Front. If a BJP member really thought that the party could get a majority, he was dreaming. Five years of course is a long time, and time is like a perennial river which flows on and on and opportunities are bound to offer themselves for the Opposition.

CAA Doubts in Assam

THE CITIZENSHIP (AMENDMENT) Act, 2019, brings nightmares to the Assamese people for fear of further arrival of Bengali-speaking people from Bangladesh. The immigrants may be legal but the dilution of the local culture and the threat to the political voice of the Assamese would be about the same, regardless of how good the newcomers may be.

Before offering the remedy, two points need to be made. One, the Assamese, whether Adivasi or the more modernised ones, are dead scared of being outnumbered by the Bengali-speaking people, whether Hindu or Muslim. Merely assuring the people that protecting their culture is as much the Centre's concern as securing the culture of the entire country, would not satisfy them.

Unless one has lived or frequently travelled in Assam, it is difficult to appreciate what nightmares the Assamese see when they think of infiltration, legal or otherwise. They are a gentle people with a soft peace-loving nature. They have their own festivals. They were gifted by nature with plenty of land and even more rivers and water. They do not have to work too hard for survival. The climate is mostly warm and humid, and not very congenial for hard work. They are not competitive by nature and understandably shudder at the fear of this ethos being disturbed by outsiders.

Believe it not, until two decades ago it was a popular impression that the Congress strategy for winning elections in Assam was "Ali, Coolie and Bengali". Coolie implied the tea garden workers and their families. Ali and Bengali are self-explanatory; they are mostly people who had over the years immigrated into Assam. Even the tea garden workers were Adivasis brought from Jharkhand and neighbouring areas to plant and pluck the leaves. To this day, it is difficult to find an original Assamese who is a plucker in a tea garden. In sum and substance, the Congress depended on settlers from outside to win a majority vote.

In 1947, MA Jinnah nearly convinced the British rulers that Assam was a Muslim-majority province and should go to Pakistan. Sheikh Mujibur Rahman, in his book *Eastern Pakistan*, stated that the tribals were not only not Hindus but also unfit for civilised life. The generally vague conclusion of the sympathisers for Pakistan was that Eastern Bengal and Assam should be combined into one province as was the case under the first partition of Bengal by Viceroy Lord Curzon in 1905. Fortunately, it was undone by 1911. Lord Pethic Lawrence, Secretary of State for India in the Atlee government of 1945-49, also swallowed this theory about an amalgamation of the two.

The deception was almost done when Gopinath Bordolai, the Assam Congress leader rushed out to persuade those in power and influence that the Jinnah contention was untrue. As a result, Assam was saved for India except for Sylhet district, which had a Muslim majority. Any wonder that the Assamese are afraid of allowing illegal migrants to settle? Incidentally, until 1874, Assam was a part of the Bengal Presidency. It was then separated and placed under the rule of a Chief Commissioner. To make Assam a viable separate province, three Bengali-speaking districts of the Presidency—Goalpara, Sylhet and Cachar were merged into the new province. That is how Assam began to host Bengalis as well as Muslims. The going of Sylhet to East Pakistan in 1947 relieved this pressure to an extent.

Assam, however, can ill afford to host more immigrants; the Assamese population is so small. The recent Citizenship (Amendment) Act is a major irritant for them especially since what was discovered in 1979. Some young men discovered in the electoral rolls of the Mangaldai assembly constituency that many a voter was an obvious infiltrator. In order to spread the protest and try and stop such distortion of the electoral rolls of the State, the All Assam Students Union (AASU) was formed. Some members also went on to establish the Assam Ganatantra Parishad (AGP), a major political party. A few members took to terrorism under the name of the United Liberation Front of Assam (ULFA).

The solution to a potentially very serious national problem would lie in making the Cachar region a separate Union Territory having no special political connection with Assam. Cachar has a population of some 40 lakh of whom a little over half are Hindu; fewer than two percent are Christian and the rest Muslim. More or less, all speak and write Bengali. Its economy is viable especially with the help of over a hundred tea gardens which produce five crore kilograms of tea worth some 800 crore rupees annually. That would separate some 16 percent of the total Assam population, virtually all of them Bengali, whether Muslim or Hindu, a great relief to the Assamese. This is the one sure way to bring happiness to the Assamese people after at least a century. In any case, the Cacharis would be pleased at being semi-independent with Silchar becoming a mini *rajdhani*.

Democracy

IN THE CURRENT political scenario, there is no effective national opposition to the ruling BJP. There are intellectuals like Kapil Komireddi who believe that democracy in India is in danger unless a viable Opposition is created before the 2024 general election. Otherwise, democracy may be replaced by some form of dictatorship. While Komireddi seems to lay the blame at the door of Congress Vice-President Rahul Gandhi for this lacuna, in the humble opinion of this writer, blaming the scion of the Nehru dynasty alone for the lack of a viable Opposition would be wrong.

It is instructive to have a look at our post-independence history. Jawaharlal Nehru was Prime Minister from 1947 to 1964, a good 17 years, continuously. The Chinese invasion of 1962 and our defeat was a national shame, not because we lost, but for the reasons why we had to endure a defeat and the way our valorous troops suffered. The loss was not as much military as it was a case of our soldiers being misled and betrayed by a careless political leadership.

Soon after August 1947, Nehru had told the interim Commander-in-Chief of the Indian Army, General William Lockhart, "India is a peaceful country and therefore does not need an army. The police are sufficient to protect us". The result of such thinking played out on the ground too, as our armed forces were treated like pseudo-policemen. But by November 1962, Nehru panicked in the aftermath of the Chinese invasion. His favourite general BM Kaul had sent our troops up to 16,000 feet altitude in NEFA (today's Arunachal Pradesh) in cotton uniforms, one ordinary pullover and WWII .303 Lee Enfield bolt action rifles. The shoes given to them were the brown version of tennis ones and no gloves were provided to them.

When Nehru was told that there was a strong possibility of the enemy entering Assam pretty soon, he felt it was his duty to tell the local people that their state was in danger, implying that it was going to fall into Chinese hands. He seemed to be weeping on the All India Radio. Fortunately, on the night between 20 and 21 November, the Chinese declared a unilateral ceasefire.

In the meantime, many members of Parliament were clamouring for the government's resignation, but Nehru paid no heed to calls for his ouster. When the pressure became too much to ward off, he told his Defence Minister VK Krishna Menon to resign. Menon went into oblivion, but Nehru, under whose leadership India had suffered a shameful military reverse, batted on for a year and a half until he died in May 1964. The spirit of democracy demanded that the prime minister too should have resigned. A decade later, Indira Gandhi went as far as declaring a national Emergency instead of resigning in 1975, following an Allahabad High Court verdict that held her election itself to be unlawful. Her dictatorial regime of the next 19 months, with its attendant banishment of democracy itself, is much written about. This was followed by her humiliating defeat in the next general election in March 1977. Should she have done what she did? Was that democracy? Why then blame Rahul Gandhi alone? He did resign as President of the Congress following its second humiliating rout in the 2019 Lok Sabha elections, and has not returned to the presidentship since then.

This is not to say that no change is required at all. It is for the other members of the Congress to hold a meeting and decide what is necessary to be done. What the 23 letter-writing members—now dubbed the G-23—have written is like employees appealing to their employer or owner of the party. If that is their equation with the Gandhi family, it has to be said that they consider the latter to be indispensible, in which case, the party members should quietly accept what the Gandhis do or lump it. There is nothing else to be done. One has to recall that when Nehru did not budge despite India's humiliation at the hands of China, or when Indira Gandhi threw out democracy itself with the Emergency in 1975, no Congressman revolted or took a public stand. Surely quite a few Congressmen must have disagreed with both or either of these situations. As it happened, the Congress endured both the crises.

The younger generation might or might not be aware that after PV Narasimha Rao ceased to be prime minister following the party's defeat in the 1996 general elections, there were months when it was feared that the party was falling apart and Sonia Gandhi's leadership was the only way to keep it united. She did bring the Congress back to power and ruled by proxy for ten years from 2004-14. She was nothing more than Rajiv Gandhi's spouse, had no experience of political life and is not even an ethnic Indian. Yet, her leadership, or more accurately absolute control, proved finally that the Gandhi dynasty owns the Congress. Rahul and Priyanka are the progeny of Rajiv Gandhi; take it or leave it. With its boundless brand equity, it may blossom again or may not. If one does not feel optimistic, one should move to another party but should not complain.

Coming to the larger issue, dynasties do not augur well for the life of a democracy. A national Opposition which is truly a political set-up with an inner party democracy is the ideal. In its absence, one needs the party in power to be broad minded enough to ensure governance by consensus, as is the case with the present party. No policy can be supported by a hundred percent of the electorate but it should have an acceptance of a comfortable majority of the people.

It is also not a coincidence that modern democracy has come naturally to countries with Anglo-Saxon roots. England (later Britain) made a beginning in the year 1215 by making King John sign the Magna Carta (Great Charter), which mainly enshrined the rule of law. Nothing substantial happened until 1781 when the USA wrote a novel Constitution encompassing a distinct separation of power between the legislature, executive and the judiciary. Canada and Australia, being dominions of the British Empire, adopted the path ploughed by Britain.

France has stuck to democracy after writing a secular constitution in the year 1905. Germany tried democracy from 1920 to 1934, followed by the unfortunate interlude of Adolf Hitler and his Nazis. The country again returned to a democratic system after World War II and has stayed firmly on that path. The Scandinavian countries have been democratic; they are a part of the Anglo-Saxon family.

Some countries call themselves democratic because they have elections, but that is not enough. Even Pakistan claims to be a democracy. Turkey has an elective system monitored by its army. The bald truth is that countries of this kind merely go through the motions of a democratic exercise like elections. India, though, is one nation which has been sincere in its democracy.

Interfaith Marriages

AT MY NIECE'S wedding in a church, the officiating priest began by declaring: "Marriage is a union, divine and indivisible". This is a succinct way of expressing that marriage is a sacrament; no breaking until death does the couple apart.

The Dictionary of Islam by Thomas Patrick Hughes (published by Rupa & Co) calls marriage a *nikah*, a word that in its literal sense means a contract. It is a contract till the husband wants. He can divorce his wife at pleasure by giving a notice of three months. The wife does not have this privilege. If she wants to separate, she has to follow the procedure of *khula*, which entails finding a *qazi* and convincing him under the rules of *fiqh* or dogmatic theology of Muslims.

If a Muslim man and Hindu woman fall in love, it should be recommended that they marry under the Special Marriage Act, which does not have unequal rights nor requires the woman to change her religion and possibly her name; whereas a *nikah* insists that both partners be of the same religion—

actually Muslim. If the man does not wish to divorce, he can take another wife.

It is rare to find an interfaith marriage where the bride is a Muslim and the groom a Hindu. Perhaps the reason is that it is impermissible for a non-Muslim man to marry a Muslim woman, as he would have legal authority over her. The tenets of Islam say that God doesn't allow non-Muslims to have authority over Muslims. A Muslim man can marry a non-Muslim woman, but not vice-versa. This seems unfair, but the Islamic rationale is that a non-Muslim man will not respect his Muslim wife's faith. These tenets also hold that while Muslims believe in all Prophets of God and respect them, a non-Muslim does not return the favour. A non-Muslim husband might not explicitly express this, but a Muslim wife cannot expect her husband to respect her faith. Muslims believe in only the revealed religions of the Book, not other religions.

Some time ago, the celebrated IAS couple Tina Dabi and Athar Amir filed for divorce in Jaipur, two years after they tied the nuptial knot. Their love story and marriage in 2018 had made national headlines. IAS officer Tina Dabi saying she had married a Muslim man and was now separated from her husband Khan after two years of marriage, went viral in a video. Dabi alleged her husband tortured her to wear a *burqa,* convert to Islam, read namaz and adopt Khan in her name.

Even without divorce, a Muslim male can marry up to four wives at a time; with divorce, there is no limit on the number of wives he can have. Hinduism and Christianity insist on only one wife. For marrying a Muslim boy, a girl must understand many things she may face. If the boy is Muslim, his faith enjoins upon him to produce as many children as possible, so that they achieve demographic preponderance. This is borne out by the Hadith (The Traditions, the second holy book after the Quran) according to *The Dictionary of Islam* by Hughes. Concerned Hindus understandably use the word jihad in this context.

It is time to stop romanticising interfaith marriages blindly. Marrying Muslim men does entail legal outcomes for non-Muslim women. Today's political discourse tends to ignore arguments of those who have issues with such marriages. Selective quoting and presentation of only particular views as acceptable does not help the cause of any informed debate. Current secular outrage over interfaith marriages souring is focused on romanticising interfaith marriages themselves and treating all such alliances as the same, which they regrettably are not.

The rights of women marrying under the Hindu Marriage Act or Special Marriage Act vary greatly from the rights of those who wed as per the Sharia. Under Sharia, non-Muslim women have to convert to Islam first because this is the condition for marriage under Sharia. Thus, any non-Muslim woman marrying a Muslim man instantly forfeits all her rights as she transits from a legal regime with more rights to one with fewer rights. This is not reversible, as Islam does not permit apostasy. Many women who convert for the sake of getting married believing they can continue to practise their faith are quickly belied of this notion; the faith they marry into doesn't permit this. Moreover, Hindus hold marriage to be a sacrament where even divorce is considered an anathema (though allowed legally). Under Sharia, it is only a contract where a man can divorce his wife orally and instantly by simply saying *talaq* thrice (till it was banned). This is the chasm between the two worlds.

Non-Muslim women must be made aware of these consequences. The blind eulogy and advocacy of interfaith marriages and pretending that all such alliances are of the same nature is dishonesty. Rosy and romanticised pictures of interfaith marriages carry the serious propensity of harming non-Muslim women, who might make hasty and misinformed decisions only to repent and suffer.

Love Jihad

IN KERALA, TRADITIONALLY the Christians, especially the Church, have been politically sympathetic to their Abrahamic siblings. They have not generally leaned towards the Hindus. However, two or three years ago, a bishop had publically said that in 50 years Kerala would become a Muslim state. Now again, PC George, an MLA of the Janapaksham (Secular) Party of Erattupetta has complained against misconduct by some Muslims. The discord between the legislator George and the Muslim electorate in the constituency, which reached its peak during the recent Assembly elections, continues to simmer even after polling.

The latest episode was played out on 13th April with PC George openly stating that love jihad is prevalent in Erattupetta. "There is love jihad at Erattupetta and 47 girls from the region, including 12 Hindu girls, have so far fallen victim to the practice", he alleged. He said the recent instances in which girls from Aniyilappu and Thikkoyi went missing were indeed cases of love jihad. "This was what happened in the case of Jesna [Maria James] as well," George said.

The statement takes a cue from his controversial speech at Thodupuzha when he abruptly raised the love jihad issue. The speech drew sharp reactions from various quarters and invited a police complaint, but George stood his ground. Observers, however, regard his latest remarks as a continuation of his widening discord with the Muslim electorate since the Parliament elections of 2019. The legislator has been accused of engaging in anti-Muslim rhetoric with an eye on Hindu and Christian votes. Addressing media persons later, he confirmed receipt of tacit support from the Bharatiya Janata Party.

Hardly a month passes when someone or the other does not cry out aloud about the evil design of the Sangh parivar for the establishment of a Hindu rashtra. A Hindu theocracy is a contradiction in terms, but the argument will be more convincing if it is presented after first facing the loud cry frontally.

In India, there is only one outstanding example of a self-proclaimed Hindu state and that too in recent times. A Japanese scholar, Koji Kawashima, has researched and recorded the experience of Travancore between 1858 and 1936 in his book *Missionaries and a Hindu State* (OUP; 1998). The study was funded by two Japanese foundations called Yoshida and Morita and supervised by a British professor, David Arnold. It can, therefore, be relied upon as an impartial and objective work on an Indian state. The following excerpts from the books help to describe Travancore's state Hinduism as well as how the non-Hindu citizens were treated:

> In India, the kingly duties have been called *rajadharma*,

> which can be defined as the obligation of the ruler to protect dharma or to secure peace, prosperity, justice and order in the kingdom. Of these duties, protection of the gods and their temples was perhaps the most important. As a servant of Sri Padmanabha, the Maharaja of Travancore observed a number of rituals, most of which were started by Martanda Varma in the mid-18th century. Travancore had a large number of non-Hindus, particularly Syrian Christians. In 1875, Christians formed about 20 percent of the population, and Muslims six percent. These different religions seem to have coexisted and largely integrated into the Hindu state in pre-modern Travancore. One of the principal reasons for this coexistence was a semi-official state policy of religious tolerance.

Regarding this, Lieutenants Ward and Conner, who surveyed Travancore and Cochin from 1816 to 1820, state that Christianity was fully acknowledged by the chief authorities in those states and, whether from their justice or indifference, does not appear to have been exposed to persecution. J Knowles, a well-known missionary, stated in 1898 that the Travancore state was conspicuous by its tolerance of non-Hindu religions. In fact, Hindu kings gave the Syrians privileges and honours that distinguished them as a high caste. The Syrians themselves attempted to have the support of the king when there was a dispute over ecclesiastical power within their church. Also, as the American historian Leslie Brown pointed out, Syrian Christians joined in many Hindu festivals.

Clearly, the Hindu state of Travancore did not discriminate against the followers of other faiths. The overriding evidence of this is the present population profile of Kerala a large part of which had belonged to Travancore. Incidentally, the other major states of what is now called Kerala were Cochin and Malabar. Both were ruled by Hindu monarchs. As far as religious tolerance was concerned, they were similar to Travancore. In fact, all the three were so tolerant that they freely allowed change of religion. Today, 20 percent of Keralites are Christian and a similar percentage Muslim. Why is, therefore, a periodical outcry against the Sangh parivar's reported wish to establish a Hindu rashtra? Assuming this was true, no one has any need to fear going by the prototype as represented by Travancore.

The implication is that the Hindu ethos has no tangible model of the state. It is true that Rama was looked upon as an ideal king. The *Mahabharata* discusses the three prime duties of a king, namely, protecting the borders of the state, ensuring justice, law and order for the people and selecting a competent successor to the throne.

Bhishma, the grandsire of the Kuru Dynasty instructs Yudhishthira about the ideal judicial and legal set-up for the kingdom. He also speaks of a strict penal system and insists on the right kind of punishment for crimes. Also addressing Yudhishthira, Bhishma explains the duties of a king, especially in the context of the economy as well as defence. Sri Krishna's wisdom is wide-ranging as well as fascinating. The *Bhagavad Gita* is a theory of life, valid eternally. Krishna's guidance through the epic has a great deal to teach about strategy and practice for life as well as the battlefield. Yet, there is no religious theology on how a state must be run and certainly not anything on a Hindu polity. Evidently, even in those ancient times, worship was kept far away from the conduct of the state. Otherwise, somewhere or the other we should be able to come across the theory of a Hindu state.

Kautilya's *Arthashastra* is far more comprehensive about how a kingdom should be run. Nevertheless, even if one were to build the model of a state on the basis of the details, there would be nothing Hindu about a Kautilyan policy. To the best of my knowledge, there is no mention of either worship or religion in *Arthashastra.* The model would be strictly secular in the original European sense of the state being separate from the church.

Coming to recent times, Mahatma Gandhi did talk about Ram Rajya whose model he did not construct on paper. Nevertheless, it was his idea of an ideal state. One essential sentence from Gandhi needs to be quoted here: "By Ram Raj, I do not mean Hindu Raj. By Ram Raj I mean Divine Raj, the kingdom of God. For me, Ram and Rahim are the same deity". Even then, when a non-Hindu hears the word Ram, he takes it for granted that the concept is that of a Hindu state.

Same-Sex Marriages

A SAME-SEX marriage is novel and different from the traditional sacramental or contractual coming together of a man and a woman. It is a union between two persons, between two men or two women, legitimised by religion or by law. It enables the couple to bear children who are, therefore, legitimate. Giving birth to children or procreation is a duty for the perpetuation of the human race. A primary function of marriage is legitimate procreation.

There are men and women who live together without being married, especially in Europe, but hesitate to produce children, while there are others who do not hesitate. In Gujarat's Vadodara city some 30 years ago, a leading lawyer introduced a novelty called *maîtree karar* or a friendship contract. It laid down in a legal document all the necessary conditions about the future of the man's property and assets as well as other commitments. Being from a traditional orthodox family, he had been married when very young. Subsequently he was educated as a lawyer while his wife remained uneducated.

The mental or intellectual gulf between the two became wide. Their two children remained with the wife but he maintained them all, though he lived separately with a younger lady whom he had befriended. To assure her future security she requested for a contract and the lawyer acceded. Following their example, several others in Gujarat adopted this contract method. Seldom did the parties to the contract procreate; in that they did not fulfill their duty to nature.

Two young ladies, one very distantly related to me and the other of Chinese origin were both residing in Canada at the time. They became such close friends that they got married. In due course, the Indian lady met an Englishman, a bachelor, who had a great desire to have children. With the consent of the Chinese spouse, the Indian girl had two children. A few years later, the Chinese lady also met someone with whom there grew a desire to have children. The same-sex couple and their children stay together whereas the fathers visit them according to mutual convenience.

However odd these incidents may appear to normal or traditional persons, a free society should allow people to do what they want. But that does not mean that the current laws should have to accommodate new oddities. For such people the legislatures should make separate laws so that the concerned pioneers do not feel insecure or outside the pale of society. Merely for illustrating my contention, let same-sex marriages be under a law called a unity-contract or anything else but not marriage.

Experts may have several explanations of what in the

old days would have been called perversities, but are now sympathised with as abnormalities. In my own lay observation, homosexuality develops normally due to the denial of access or exposure to the other gender. Boarding schools occasionally report such cases and lately, irregularities have also come to the surface in churches. Again, going by my experience of being an only child, I suffered from extreme shyness in mixing with girls. I somehow had the notion that if I took the initiative, the girl might misunderstand and feel that I was taking liberties, which was so wrong.

Another unusual experience I witnessed was of my aunt. She fell in love with an older doctor. He was earlier married in his village before completing his studies. In due course, he and his wife had three healthy children. The mental or intellectual gulf between the spouses had grown considerably. The doctor's problem was similar to that of the lawyer of Vadodara. He responded to my aunt; they became friends and remained so for years. When I was about eight years old, they came to see my grandfather for permission to marry. If he did not object, they would take a train to Goa and get married there. The reason was that the Bombay Provincial law had prohibited bigamy by 1945, whereas the Goan rules permitted it.

They went to Goa, got married and all lived together under one roof. That is the two wives, six children and the doctor husband who happily survived till he was 83. As I grew up, I awoke to a contradiction in the Bombay Provincial law. My aunt and uncle had to go to Goa to escape the ban on bigamy but thousands of others are in law exempted from it and permitted the privilege of polygamy. This discrimination is now prevalent across India. Either polygamy should be allowed for all but under a distinct, separate law, or preferably it should be prohibited for all citizens of the country. But different privileges to different people under the law is discriminatory and wrong.

Delayed Justice

THERE ARE REPEATED mentions in the print media about the astronomical number of cases which are pending in the Supreme Court, the various High Courts and the lower courts. The reported numbers are close to four crore cases in the apex court, the high court and the lower courts. The explanation for this state of affairs usually is a shortage of judges in most courts. What is to be done, except request the government to expedite appointments? Overall, the legal fraternity is responsible and intelligent but it has not occurred to anyone influential that the system is defective.

Foremost ought to be the question of why so many adjournments are sought, and given freely by the courts? Not only freely, but also free of charge. In other words, the court's time and facilities including the time of judges is misused. The court fees are paid according to the prescribed list, but the fees are listed regardless of whether a case gets over in two or three hearings or takes 30 hearings over several years. For the sake of freedom, I concede that litigants should have the basic right to seek adjournments. But on their part, they must be enjoined with a duty to pay some rate of fee for each adjournment. Say, the court fee to be paid for filing a suit is one lakh, an adjournment should cost the side seeking it about Rs 50,000 or at least Rs 25,000. The habit of adjournment seeking would come down drastically.

As a layman who has to litigate from time to time since I run a school, I can say that litigants have a fancy for famous, known and popular advocates. Such advocates are busy because they argue many briefs simultaneously and also in out-stations like Chennai, Jabalpur etc. At times, the same distinguished advocate has to appear in the Supreme Court for a matter. My experience is that a litigant should choose an advocate who would have the leisure to study the matter thoroughly and be available to argue the matter, rather than being in Chennai or elsewhere that particular day. All these factors should begin to count once litigants realise the price of their advocate's absence.

Our school had an unusual experience in one of its initial cases in the Delhi High Court. The Advocate-on-Record suggested we go in for a particular advocate, who was not only very capable but enjoyed the respect of the High Court judge. The expense would perhaps be double. We did as advised and the conference with the advocate was fixed for the Saturday preceding the Monday, when our matter was listed. The advocate could not make it that day, so he postponed it to Sunday. That too proved to be very busy for him. Then we were told we would have a quick meeting on Monday morning at 10 am in the lobby of the Court. We waited until 10.30 when news came that the advocate had had to go to the Company

Law Board on an urgent matter. By 11 am, our matter was slated to come up. So I asked a younger lawyer (who had never before argued in Court) to represent us. When the time came, my young advocate stood up shakily. Before he could say much, the judge said, "Oh yes, this type of a matter was decided by the High Court only about two months ago. Has anyone got a copy of that judgment?" We had the copy but in his nervousness the young man had forgotten to present it. The moment he produced it, the judge said, "Fine, leave it with me and I will write my order in a few days". It eventually was a victory for the school! Although it was unusual, such flukes do not succeed often.

Apart from adjournments, another cause of delay is the freedom of advocates arguing for an unlimited length of time. Some hearings go on for hours. Why shouldn't the judge, in consultation with the advocates of the two sides, fix say half an hour or 45 minutes for each side? If one of the advocates crosses his time limit, he may but at the cost for every five minutes extra, rather like a taxi meter. The charge for every extra five minutes should be a standard one. Long arguments usually contain repetitions, although the advocates' explanation is to make the judges understand their viewpoint as if they are not educated or lack a modicum of common sense. Nevertheless, this suggestion does not take away the freedom to argue at unlimited length.

If the plea is a shortage of judges, it should not be difficult to appoint more. If and when there occurs a shortage of space, a second shift can be introduced. The court could begin at 8 am and go on without a break until 1 pm. The second shift could commence at around 1.30 pm and go on until 6 in the evening. Advocates can be found as there is no dearth of them.

Appeal upon appeal is yet another phenomenon that causes delay. When I was in college in the 1950s, I knew several law students who told me that the Supreme Court was essentially a court of final appeal, mainly for constitutionally significant matters. It admitted some matters of high importance like fundamental rights or issues, which some provinces were concerned about. Later I found that cases which began in Small Causes Courts like landlords wanting their tenants to pay higher rents or vacate their premises would also reach the Supreme Court. Think of the layers of courts that the matter must have crossed and climbed before reaching the apex court to finally decide whether the tenant should pay Rs 6,000 per month or quit the flat he occupies. The suggestion to cut out such traffic is to allow appeals only up to the two higher courts. There may be many tribunals for specific trades or professions to free the normal courts. But here again the appeals, if any, should not extend beyond one higher court.

Most litigants continue to have faith in the higher judiciary as long as they are not asked for under-the-table money to win their case. In other words, in the popular mind, the reliability of a court is judged by its integrity. Delays are a matter of debate, but have not yet become a criterion of the judiciary's efficacy.

But times are changing, and a point may be reached when courts would begin to be judged as much for their efficiency and quickness of justice, as for their honesty. I know of three cases of shoplifting in London, which were decided between 11.00 in the morning and noon. In two of the cases, the well-known Old Bailey's Court gave the litigants some kind of an informal bail in lieu of depositing their passports as a surety. At four o' clock, the matter was taken up and the fines in the two cases were 100 pounds and 175 pounds sterling. In the third case, justice was even quicker, as the young man was made to sit in the court and was fined 40 pounds, without availing of the services of a lawyer. The matter was decided by 4.30 pm, in half an hour.

The reason for quoting these instances is to bring to notice how speedy justice can be.

On Sri Lanka and the Andamans

TWO COMMUNITIES NOT being able to coexist is a perennial problem in the Indian subcontinent. An old saying goes, "*Do talwaren ek myan mein nahi reh sakti*", meaning two swords cannot fit into one scabbard. The problem began by being underscored in our own country India, which was divided into Pakistan for Muslims and India for the rest. MA Jinnah argued that Hindus and Muslims were two separate nations and could not coexist in one country. The first leader to push this two-nation theory was Sir Syed Ahmad of Aligarh fame.

Some UP Muslims believed their new country Pakistan was a New Medina. Muslims in the western wing despised the eastern Bengalis as inferior, short and dark. Their economy was exploited from day one. Jinnah visited Dacca early in 1948 and peremptorily told university students that Urdu alone would be Pakistan's national language. Bengali, which they were proud of, was not in the reckoning. The two wings were daggers drawn from 1948; the clash came in 1971, less than 24 years after the New Medina's birth. In December that year they separated and Bangladesh was born.

Thus India was divided into three. Now we hear that the people of Sindh wish to separate. This separatist movement is called Jio Sindh. They find it difficult to exist under the yoke of the dominant Punjabis. Baluchistan is another unhappy province which was partly British India and partly the princely state of Kalat. It had an embassy in Karachi until 1948 when Pakistan forcibly took it over. The Pathans of the NWFP with their main city Peshawar have always wished to unite with all Pathans in Afghanistan, though this demand is dormant now.

With Sri Lanka, it is an old problem. I visited my in-laws in Colombo in 1964 as they wanted to introduce me to their society in the city where they had lived and worked for 32 years. In the course of my four days, there arose the question of who would be the next managing director of the British Ceylon Corporation, a British firm similar to the one we had at Kanpur, the British India Corporation until the early 1960s. My father-in-law said that one Ramaswamy, a local Tamil was the best choice but was unlikely to get the promotion. The prize was likely to go to DM Pereira as he was a Sinhala. The current board of directors was largely British headed by a distinguished gentleman called Singleton Salmon. There was no partiality in the company but the emerging milieu in Colombo was such.

My father-in-law explained that the Sinhalas were an overwhelming majority; they were an easy-going, fun-loving Buddhist people. They were jealous of the Tamils who were serious at work, were more efficient and performed well. There had developed a wedge between the two groups as far back as then. Their differences were bound to explode sooner or later.

The fact that the people of Tamil Nadu have a soft corner in their hearts for their Sri Lankan brethren is natural but that makes Sinhalas suspect Indian intentions from time to time. When Rajiv Gandhi was India's Prime Minister and President Jayawardene headed Sri Lanka, we sent the IPKF military force to help the Tamils. Instead of helping them, we only killed them and left the Sinhalas alone. This indicates that our governments have mostly not understood Sri Lankan affairs.

Colombo's rulers smile at New Delhi and pretend to be friendly although they feel that the faraway yellow giant is less dangerous than the Indian giant only 40 km to their north. They did appreciate the IPKF's help for some time; thereafter it became a distant memory. Sri Lanka appears to have erred in owing China all the money for upgrading the Hambantota port as well as a highway from Colombo to Galle and further south. If Sri Lanka cannot repay the loan in time, these may be taken over as Chinese property. Yet Colombo would rather deal with Beijing than New Delhi. This mentality is likely to continue indefinitely until India takes a drastic step to relieve the Sinhalas of their Tamil suspicions. From the Indian point of view, there is the fear, however remote, that one day the Chinese may convert Sri Lanka into a yellow colony.

What should New Delhi do? Can it consider whether we can offer a transfer of willing Sri Lankan Tamils to the Andaman Islands? They are a community of four million people, mainly in the Jaffna area in the northeast of Sri Lanka with some scattered across the east of the island. The Andamans occupy about 9,000 square km with only about four lakh people. Not all Sri Lankan Tamils are likely to accept the transfer. For those willing, Sri Lanka should pay a total Rs 2 lakhs per head towards resettlement, conveyance costs and compensation. This means several billion rupees for Sri Lanka to borrow or somehow fork out, but a small cost for solving their greatest problem. India's advantage would be populating the Andaman Islands, which makes Tamils' survival safer, Tamil Nadu happier and puts Indo-Sri Lankan relations in a permanently suspicion-free space.

Lesson from Gyan Vapi

IT WAS THE year 1927; one Abdul Rashid murdered Swami Shradhanand, the successor of Swami Dayananda Saraswati, in his sickbed. The killer was arrested and tried. The British government then had no qualms about the religions of the two men. Jawaharlal Nehru's friend Asaf Ali, a distinguished advocate, took up Rashid's brief. The Court, nevertheless, sentenced him to death as it was a cold-blooded murder. The *janaza* (funeral) was attended by several thousands of Rashid's sympathisers, but there was no riot or communal disturbance. Had any riot taken place the government would not have flinched from suppressing it. If the British inclined to be soft, they could not have ruled an empire for a total of 190 years. That empire had 40 crore Indians, with the white men from the British Isles being never more than a hundred thousand.

Take the case of Ayodhya. The All India Personal Law Board lost its long litigation eventually ending in the Supreme Court; not a single Muslim stabbed a Hindu. In Ayodhya itself, everyone was in favour including the local Muslims, on the grounds that a temple would vastly increase the number of pilgrims coming and the city's economy would flourish. If at all any violence took place, it was because of the firing earlier by Mulayam Singh Yadav's police in 1990. The Mulayam regime resorted to indiscriminate shooting, not sparing even boys. No violence occurred owing to any mischief by a Muslim. It has been my consistent experience that when confronted with facts, most Muslims are willing to accept them. A member of the Muslim Personal Law Board confided to me that the Board fought the Ayodhya issue in court for so long merely to stall Hindu demands for other temples-turned-mosques.

Years ago, the chief of Jamaat-e-Islami visited Delhi for a few days and also spent a couple of hours at my place. His explanation for Islamic conquerors replacing temples with mosques was that they wished to declare to the people that a change of regime had taken place. A Hindu raja had been replaced by a Muslim sultan or *badshah*. In reply I asked if a Hindu prime minister took over in a Hindu-majority country, would it be fair to reverse the situation? Should not the mosques be replaced by temples? Again, as a true Muslim, the Jamaat chief promptly responded that if that was the prime minister's and his people's desire, so be it.

In 1961, while delivering an Azad Memorial Lecture, visiting British historian Arnold Toynbee who was especially invited by Jawaharlal Nehru, said: "In the course of the first Russian occupation of Warsaw, the Russians had built an Eastern Orthodox Christian Cathedral in the city that had been the capital of the once independent Roman Catholic Christian country, Poland. The Russians had done this to give the Poles a continuous ocular demonstration that the Russians were now the masters. After the re-establishment of Poland's independence in 1918 about a hundred years later, the Poles pulled this cathedral down. I do not blame the Polish government for having pulled down the Russian church. The purpose for which the Russians had built it had not been religious but political, and the purpose had also been intentionally offensive". Before reaching Delhi, Sir Arnold had taken a boat ride on the Ganga and had noticed Aurangzeb's mosque on the bank with two very tall minarets. He said at his lecture that he was surprised that this mosque was still standing even after the partition of India.

To come back to the point, should not a crime be punished commensurately? If the criminal had gotten away at the time of committing the crime, should he not be apprehended and punished when it is possible to do so later? If the wrongdoer has passed away, at least the act of crime should be reversed. What is the meaning of justice otherwise? And where would be the rule of law? Since 2014, quite a few intellectuals have been protesting that democracy in India is in danger and that liberals have no future in this country. Well, here is their opportunity to firm up democracy whose first foundation is the rule of law. One only has to read the Magna Carta of English King John.

Some scholars have expressed fears of communal riots. How many riots have taken place since 2014? It is true that recently there have been a few skirmishes at Bangalore and there was a major riot in northeast Delhi when ex-President Trump was on a visit to India. Otherwise, the scorebook as far as riots are concerned has been negative over the last seven years. In any case, how can a court of law or a government shun the enforcement of justice merely due to fear of riots?

It is well-recorded that the Kashi Vishwanath temple was destroyed on the orders given by Aurangzeb after his crowning. Fortunately, a part of its front got left out and has survived as a part of the mosque. Where people now worship Lord Shiva was built by the great Holkar Queen Ahilyabai in the 18th century. If, therefore, the Gyan Vapi mosque underwent some changes according to historical facts, no Muslim would have any objection.

Management and Countries

AN AIRCRAFT HIJACKING isn't an ideal instance to dwell on regarding the significance of management. Nonetheless, there is one such episode that offers crucial lessons on how important management is, not only in dealing with crises, but also in running a country. I refer to the hijacking of Indian Airlines flight IC-814 travelling from Kathmandu to Delhi in December 1999. The flight, with 178 passengers and eleven crew members on board had been hijacked by five armed men. Denied permission in Lahore, Pakistan, the plane landed in nearby Amritsar at around 7 pm. The hijackers demanded the release of 36 Islamist terrorists then held in Indian jails and a ransom of 200 million dollars.

Prime Minister Vajpayee was mid-air, returning to Delhi from an official tour. In the prime minister's absence, a Crisis Management Group or CMG had been set up with senior officials and the heads of intelligence agencies. The cabinet secretary was formally in charge. The CMG scurried around like a chicken whose head had been cut off. IC-814 took off from Amritsar forty-five minutes later and without it, India lost any chance of regaining control of the plane inside our own territory. An official present at that particular meeting later said: "I was present in that room, and there was nothing but indecision". In theory, the decision lay with the home minister. The hijacked flight flew to Lahore, then Dubai, and finally landed in Kandahar in Taliban-held Afghanistan. Exhausted after a week of negotiations, Vajpayee decided to release three Kashmiri terrorists in return for the passengers. The finer details are laid out in the book *Jugalbandi* by Vinay Sitapati, (published by Penguin Viking, 2020).

Just imagine what an incidence of colossal mismanagement this was. But it also underlines the fact that like corporations and enterprises, the administration of countries too needs management. No one seems to have attempted to write a thesis on how to manage a country. Lately, some hospitals and schools are being professionally managed. Mumbai's Jaslok Hospital, which began treating patients in 1973 was, to my knowledge, designed with the help of the management department of Messrs Ferguson & Co. There is a growing awareness that professional management is an indispensible pillar of any collective activity, be it business or charity. One's country needs systematic management but hardly anyone seems to have attempted such an approach. Rulers govern their countries well or badly as their abilities enable them to do.

In fact, there was no management science until World War I. The German army headquarters happened to do an exercise on the number of combatants they had and how many men were deployed to support the men who fought on the battlefield. The study revealed that the Germans had four men supporting every fighting soldier. In contrast, the British had ten men for every combatant. This meant that the British were two and a half times more expensive than the Germans in this respect. That is believed to be the beginning of the concept of management science. After the war, academicians got interested especially in the USA and gradually, management science became a subject. During World War II, studies were conducted and business management schools began coming up after the 1950s. Peter Drucker, an Austrian-American rose to fame as a management consultant.

Yet, it was the best teacher who usually became the school principal and the best professor the head of a college. In hospitals, the best doctor was made the dean. It was as though these institutions did not need specialised management. In the bargain, the best teacher or doctor got lost in the labyrinths of administration not really knowing what to do. If they showed earnestness in administration, their work would be neglected to an extent. In India, to my knowledge, Jaslok Hospital in Mumbai, before taking off had followed a consultant who had advised how to design, arrange and manage the hospital, leaving the medical aspect exclusively to the doctors. A chief accountant and chief administrator were appointed. In the bargain, the hospital worked efficiently. Gradually, the idea was picked up by others. Yet, if funds are short, a college or a school would rather put off appointing a professional manager and make do with a head clerk and call him or her manager, if the rules so require. How important management is for any group activity is not yet fully realized?

The country is far more important than individual institutions, whether corporates, schools or hospitals. Yet, there does not seem to have been any attempt at forging a science of national management. How to manage a country? Such an attempt is overwhelmingly important also because there is no qualification required to get elected to either state assemblies or Parliament. Thus, men and women who get elected are a mixed bag. They are from various backgrounds and have different levels of education.

The bureaucrats on whom the ministers tend to depend for advice, ideas and execution, are educated. But they might come armed with knowledge of languages, mathematics or philosophy. Lately, even medical doctors and engineers are joining the IAS and other services. Thus, the bureaucrats too as a group are a mixed bag and would benefit by knowing how to manage their country or parts of it. Yet, they begin work on the premise that they are competent to handle any portfolio. They are supposed to be what in Urdu are called *harfan maula* or jack of all trades.

In the absence of the knowledge, odd things occur at the cost of the country. Prime Minister Jawaharlal Nehru, on the morrow of Independence told General Lockhart, the interim head of the Indian army, "We (India) are a peaceful country and do not need an army. The police are sufficient to defend us". Nehru's Defence Minister VK Krishna Menon once got so carried away while addressing the UN General Assembly that he went on and on for hours. The following week the popular American weekly *TIME* had Menon on its cover with a caption underneath calling him a "spitting camel". India's sound case on Kashmir was thus spoilt.

When the Chinese invaded our country in 1962, Prime Minister Nehru came on the All India Radio and said: "My heart goes out to the people of Assam". In Hindi, he said, "Assam *khatre mein hai*" and seemed to be weeping. One can imagine how demoralising this must have been for the people. Rather than reassuring them, he only further depressed them, throwing them into panic.

Another prime minister, years later, was asked by a journalist as to why India was not paying sufficient attention to tourism, to which his reply was, "We are too large a country to worry about tourism!" Yet another prime minister, much touted as an economist, even went to the extent of declaring on television that the Muslims of the country must have the first claim on 15 percent of the country's resources!

The epical conversion of an ordinary city state to a little jewel of Asia is the creation of a leader Lee Kuan Yew. A 640 square km city, Singapore, was a British colonial trading post with a population of less than two million in 1959. Within a total of 40 years, its per capita income rose from 400 US dollars to 22,000! What a miracle? As Lee has written: public order, personal security, economic and social progress and prosperity are not the natural order of things especially without any natural resources. He calls this saga of Singapore "*From Third World to First*".

After World War II ended, many such third world countries sprouted. But there was and is until today no book to guide them to rise. Lee had to dream and discuss with a few colleagues to convert the ideas into a reality. Prime Minister Narendra Modi seems to govern India only with the help of his vision.

Soft State on the Path to Strength

THE NEHRUVIAN ETHOS, which had a vice-like grip over India's polity and the minds of most Indians, was a combination of socialism and secularism. Nehruvian socialism was symbolic of anti-colonialism as well as political justification for governance to be sympathetic to communists. This helped Indira Gandhi to survive as PM between her splitting the Congress in 1969 and her re-election in 1972. Secularism meant being nice to minorities and making sure that Muslims voted for the Congress.

The price of this pseudo-secularism was multifarious, but its biggest fallout was the lingering ulcer of Kashmir. India's military suffered deliberate neglect. In 1947 itself, Nehru curtly told General Lockhart (the interim army commander) that the police were adequate to protect the country. This mindset carried on till the Sonia Gandhi-Manmohan Singh decade (2004-14); not a single new weapons system was acquired, although India had inherited a depleted military.

Corruption was a perquisite for those sympathising with the party. Indira Gandhi had stamped her approval on corruption stating: "Which country in the world is free from corruption?"

The prime ministership was the monopoly of the Congress, ex-Congressmen or pro-Congressmen like Vajpayee, a mindset sustained from 1947 to 2014, seventy-seven long years. The Nehruvian ethos had sufficient time to take deep root. The best political talent went into that party. Those not in the Congress too learnt their politics—even some BJP leaders—from the Congress. This was the paradise of Nehruvianism in which many politicians, journalists and hangers-on flourished.

Imagine the consternation of the Nehruvian world when a man like Narendra Modi led the Opposition. Out of contempt, one Congressman called him a chaiwala. A few recognised him as a tornado that could blow away their paradise. They were proved right as Modi's first term itself showed. But when 2019 approached, his enemies saw a glimmer of hope. If Modi were to obtain only about 200 Lok Sabha seats, leaders within his own party might try to coalesce with Opposition members. A coalition wouldn't want Modi. Two such leaders were hopefully hovering around.

When the results gave Modi more than 300 seats, all patrons of the Nehruvian paradise were broken-hearted. Not finding anything to criticise, they grabbed mud for flinging at him. Demonetisation was "a blunder" because it destroyed the "informal" sector by which they meant the black money sector. Even scholars on TV debates repeatedly said the informal sector was "very valuable" to the Indian economy. Their stand came from estimates that 40 percent of the economy was black. Next, the historic introduction of the Goods and Services Tax

(GST)—one country one sales tax—was abused. It would earlier take a truck seven days to deliver goods but now takes only three. GST has made it dangerous to evade even income tax. Modi's adversaries called the tax "badly administered", conveniently forgetting that it was originally their idea, possibly proposed in the hope that all states wouldn't accept it. But (late) Finance Minister Jaitley succeeded in what has been a long-term boon for the economy. GST has killed a big perquisite for the denizens of Nehru's paradise.

Article 370 was deeply divisive to Indians. It carried within itself the potential of secession, not only of Kashmir but also elsewhere. It was perpetuated to keep aflame the Hindu-Muslim divide. The country was surprised to find no great reaction to this bold step. Pakistan made some noise but then kept quiet; lately its Foreign Minister too stated on the floor of the National Assembly that Article 370 is India's domestic matter.

Corruption has been significantly reduced at higher levels. Among ministers, there have been no complaints. GST has enriched the government whereas Income Tax assessments have become faceless whereby the officers remain situated afar. It is almost impossible to give a bribe and reduce one's tax bill. Black money has not disappeared, but is much reduced. With taxes low enough, payment in white is gradually becoming the habit. India is becoming digital, as is the need in the modern world.

Decades ago, Swedish scholar Gunnar Myrdal had categorised states into soft and strong. India was a soft state; Modi's governance has set it on the path of becoming a strong one. Pakistan has learnt severe lessons and Kashmir is quiet. China's behaviour has changed after Galwan. Imagine a prime minister turning up within four days at Ladakh to visit our injured soldiers in hospital and addressing our troops. What a difference that gesture made!

Another way of explaining this is that India was a half-sovereign state, whereby it was not effective and its writ did not run up to all its frontiers. This was so even domestically in some ways. Whenever a central minister was alleged to be corrupt, the prime minister would wriggle out of his responsibility terming the accused to be a coalition partner, not of the PM's party. Narendra Modi has taken India on the road to strength and full sovereignty. Those who thrived in the former erstwhile paradise do not know what has hit them.

Pandemics, Epidemics and Endemics

WE ALL KNOW that Corona is not the first pandemic to attack almost the whole world. One can only hope it neither conquers some countries nor changes the course of their history. The key to overturning a pandemic appears to be discovering the heart of it—what precisely set it off? What to destroy at the core of the disease and how to destroy it? While medical scientists and experts try to find the answers the disease runs riot.

A consolation is that Corona is by no means the first pandemic. There have been eleven predecessors and Corona is the twelveth. As far as recorded history can tell us the first calamity was caused by bubonic plague which suddenly sprouted in an Egyptian port in the sixth century. On record it has been called a pestilence; the word pandemic is a recent innovation. Plague spread far and wide, and on the way, it went to Constantinople across the Adriatic Sea, then Rome, from the Eastern to the Western Roman Empire. From early years, plague was nicknamed Black Death.

It then spread across Western Europe including Britain. Constantinople was ruled by the Emperor Justinian. He is remembered for building the Hagia Sophia, the architectural icon of the city and for centuries of an empire. The Turkish conquerors built four minarets and converted it into a mosque. Kamal Mustafa Ataturk, in the early 1920s, changed it to a museum which very recently President Erdogan has reconverted into a mosque. Incidentally, in parts of German-speaking areas, Jews were accused of poisoning the wells and, therefore, the drinking water. As a punishment, the Jews were given the choice either to convert to Christianity or face death. Those who did not convert were taken to Jewish cemeteries and collectively set on fire.

Some historians believe that the plague was a very big blow or setback to the Eastern Roman Empire which became weaker with time. No wonder that its successor, Byzantium (later Constantinople) failed to stand up to the Central Asian Turks who invaded first Anatolia and eventually Constantinople and changed its name to Istanbul. This shows how a pandemic can affect the destiny of a civilization. Christianity in the avatar of the Eastern Roman empire did not decline but the empire did. The Church is still headquartered at Istanbul with only about two to three percent Christians.

Smallpox was the next epidemic that spread from time to time and place to place. But regardless, it was a disease which used to frighten people until some decades ago. So much so, that in most parts of Asia, every infant was compulsorily vaccinated against it. Out of fear, in India the disease was worshipped as Sitala Devi and there were temples dedicated to her. It is suspected by experts that it began as a virus carried by cows or camels. These useful animals might have passed on the virus when their domestication began. The disease began, it is conjectured, about a thousand or eleven hundred years BC because it was detected in some Egyptian mummies of the time. One or two Roman emperors were recorded to have died of smallpox at the turn of the millennia. The pox did not spare Western Europe, especially Spain, from where it reached Latin America by the early years of the 16th century. A reported Spanish solution to prevent the whole family or household being infected was to demolish the whole building. This way, so many burials were avoided!

Cholera was another menace that spread mainly through water or any liquid consumed by people. It is believed to have begun in the Ganga delta. From there it travelled far and wide including Russia, especially Petersburg, then on to places in Europe early in the 19th century. The bug then crossed the Atlantic Ocean and spread for a while in the USA. The source of the epidemic of cholera was discovered by German scientists late in the 19th century. Despite this discovery, cholera also travelled east to Indonesia and south-west to some African countries. To prevent the menace of cholera all that was needed was for people to keep away from drinking doubtful water. In the West, it was nick-named Blue Death although in Kolkata, the first symptom the doctors looked for was the colour of the excreta. If it was not white, it was not cholera.

Diphtheria, Typhoid, polio, measles, influenza and yellow fever are the other endemics. Typhoid, like cholera is a water-borne disease. Polio, measles and influenza are airborne. All these are different bugs. Influenza played havoc after World War I in most parts of the world. Malaria is unique. In India it had been virtually eradicated but has come back. Evidently, in India we have allowed that particular breed of mosquito to be reborn. Incidentally, while studying modern European history, I had come across a reference to Napoleon Bonaparte having lost several thousand soldiers upon the altar of yellow fever.

Contrary to Critics, India is a Democracy

LATELY, SEVERAL OBSERVERS of democracy—Freedom House of USA, V Dem based in Sweden, and Democracy Index of UK, have commented that India may be moving towards an electoral autocracy. Such a conclusion is extremely unfair and damaging. Evidently these agencies and others are unable to appreciate India having a strong government. While the American establishment, especially the Pentagon, would like a viable ally against expansionist China, these so-called liberals prefer to see India as a permanent Third World Society.

Do they realise that India has a dominantly Hindu ethos which is intrinsically an epitome of freedom? Anyone who believes in the phenomenon of karma is a Hindu—whether he/she is a whole-time worshipper or an agonistic. No god sits in judgment over any individual or his/her community; there is no anticipation of a doomsday or an end of the world. *Anadi-ananta*—there is no beginning of life and no end according to Hindu scriptures.

Karma is reminiscent of Physics which says that for every action, there is an equal and opposite reaction. Every action by an individual, whether virtuous or vicious, is spontaneously recorded by nature or its celestial computer, as well as its reaction or *bhagya*. There is neither a single judge, nor only two alternatives for the individual namely heaven or hell.

Any assertion of a single god resembles Deductive Logic which asserts that so and so is my God and He is the only God. The corollaries that emanate from the premise are flawlessly consistent. In sharp contrast, Hinduism is a specimen of Inductive Logic. Herein lies the freedom intrinsic to Hinduism. To illustrate this contrast, say four Hindus happen to meet somewhere and discuss the subject of roses. The person from the north may say that roses are red. The southerner could assert that he has seen only white roses. The easterner may express serious disagreement and insist that roses in his region are only pink. The person from western India may say the others are wrong as roses are always yellow. After half an hour of animated argumentation, each would say: possibly in your part of the country there are other colours of roses. Someone else would propose: let us agree to disagree and request that we exchange samples of all four colours.

A member of an Abrahamic or western background, in such a controversial situation, may well declare that roses are always red; the rest must be other flowers or perhaps weeds. Just as a Jew is a Jew, the rest are gentiles. That is where conflict and war begin. Prophet Abraham when he first saw a vision said God told him to prove his bona fides by sacrificing his own son Isaac. When he was about to obey God and behead Isaac, the Almighty told him to stop and sacrifice a goat instead.

Religion in the West was thus born in violence; Prophet Moses had a much more violent experience when he freed the Israelis from the clutches of the Egyptians and brought them to Judea. Again, Jesus Christ, the son of God was brutally crucified.

When we went to Jerusalem one morning, the guide took us all to the foot of the Calvary Hill on top of which Jesus Christ was crucified. There are 14 stations or stops to the top of the hill where now stands the Church of Sepulchre where the son of God was buried. At that time I was too weak to climb so much. To please my wife, I said I would climb to station two and sit down and wait for them to return from the top. However, something in the air drew me on and on. I went up all the fourteen stations. I am not a Christian nor have I been to a missionary school. I climbed to the top of the hill and returned without feeling any extra weakness or fatigue.

In the deductive religions, there is limited scope for spirituality beyond the scriptures and places of worship. As a result, the believers tend to unite communally and fight in order to fulfill themselves collectively in the service of God. On the other hand, the inductive Hindus are dependent on individual karmas and have no pressure to unite to serve society, and in turn God. They unite only in the face of severe collective danger. They believe they are peace-loving though in the eyes of others they might seem deficient in courage. But those who believe in the deductive approach have their histories littered with violence and war.

As early as the ascension of Prophet Muhammad in 632 AD, the Caliphs initiated the conquest of the Middle-East from Morocco in the west to Iran in the east. The Moors of North Africa invaded Spain in 712 AD and reached Poitiers in France.

The Christians were also restless and soon enough, encouraged by the Vatican, went across Europe to their holy land centered in Jerusalem. In all, the Crusades were fought eight times. There was much more intra-Christian fighting. Historian Ian Morris, in his book *War*, calls it the Five Hundred Years War but it was actually longer. Eventually Britain alone conquered one-fourth of the world.

Fascism—what is it?

INDIA HAS SOME 53 recognised state parties and 8 recognised national political parties, all registered with the Election Commission at Delhi. But how many of them have we heard of? The personal differences between two politicians often results in two parties. Take the Left Front in West Bengal, which has had seven Marxist constituents—the CPI (M), CPI, Revolutionary Socialist Party, CPI (Marxist-Leninist), Forward Bloc, Forward Bloc (Marxists) and Socialist Unity Centre. But surprisingly, there is no mention of a Fascist party, based on a notable ideology which held sway in Italy, Germany, Japan and Spain during the first half of the 20th century.

In the minds of some in Europe and many in India, fascism is a dirty word, which comes in handy for abusing a political opponent. Despotism and violence are their criteria of judging this ideology. But self-declared anti-fascist Leftists conveniently forget that Russia's communist dictator Josef Stalin had over thirty million people killed between 1924 and 1953. China's record under Mao is equally brutal, as is the ruthless manner in which the Red Indians were butchered in North America.

Benito Mussolini initiated the fascist movement in March 1919 at Milan and founded the party called Partito Nazional Fascista in November 1921. The ideology sustained Italy well until 1943. Why does the very word "fascist" denote political derogation? This is reason enough to recapitulate what fascism is.

The word "fascio" means a bundle or a bunch implying unity. The movement was in response to the corruption, unemployment and the virtual economic collapse in Italy after World War I. The then prevailing socioeconomic conditions appeared to be ripe for a communist revolution and fascism was a nationalist answer to pre-empt a red takeover. Marxism was looked upon as depicting "class conflict". Capitalism still carried the stigma of "class exploitation" and was, therefore, a non-starter as a popular programme. To be effective, the answer had to be something that would prove attractive to the peasants, workers as well as their unions. This was discovered in "class collaboration" as represented by fascism.

Prof Alfredo Rocco, Minister of Justice in the Mussolini cabinet, set forth the gist of this new ideology in the course of a speech at Perugia in 1925. According to him, the society does not exist for the individual, but the individual for the society. Economic progress is a social interest and all classes of people should combine or collaborate to maximise production. The interests of the employers and that of the employed are identical. To ensure that this is practised, there must be a system of state discipline over class conflicts. Strikes and lockouts are alike illegal and punishable by heavy fines, and in certain cases, by imprisonment.

Wherever possible, the employers and workers in each industry, trade or profession were organised together in syndical associations. Where it was not possible to form such syndicates, the unions and the employers' associations remained but combined to form guilds to coordinate and ensure cordiality. If collective bargaining could not end disputes satisfactorily, they were referred to law courts assisted by experts. This is how class collaboration was conceptualised by the Fascist Party.

In practice, the economy was toned up by rearmament and public works. Soldiers were recruited in large numbers and so were workers in factories to produce arms. This would bring profits to the bourgeoisie who could then look after the proletariat well. Urban prosperity would increase demand for agricultural produce. What was left of the under-employed youth was absorbed by the armed forces. The promise to the whole nation was foreign conquests which would bring booty. The Albanian adventure and the invasion of Abyssinia (now Ethiopia) were two efforts to fulfill this promise until World War II broke out.

Another example of the practice of fascism or class collaboration, albeit on a much more limited scale, was in Spain under General Francisco Franco. Neither the Italian nor the Spanish experience is widely known in any great detail in India. What the members of the intelligentsia are familiar with are the doings of Adolf Hitler and his Nazi Party. It was founded by Hitler and his six comrades in Munich in 1920. The economic deprivation in Germany was much greater than witnessed in Italy. The country paid an exorbitant price for its defeat in World War I. The runaway inflation as well as the global depression ignited by the crash in share prices on the Wall Street in New York in 1929 made matters hot for Germany. It was widely believed that the charismatic genius of Hitler and his programme of class collaboration was more or less on the lines of Mussolini's, although on a far grander scale.

It is not suggested that any country resorts to either despotism or conquest of other countries; rather the approach of class collaboration may be tried by some Third World countries for rapid economic progress.

Israel-Hamas Scuffle

WHO HAS A superior right over Palestine or Judea? Hamas per se is an authorised organisation that represents the Arab point of view. The Israel forces are acting also on behalf of the Jewish sentiment the world over. Who provoked the current clash and why or how is a matter of detail. If only one side were to get the whole of Palestine, which side has a more valid right to the ownership of that land?

I had an opportunity to discuss this fundamental issue with a few educated Jews as well as Arabs, and also with one Israeli Christian couple when we were visiting Jerusalem some years ago. The Arab viewpoint was that we have lived in Palestine for centuries and the few Jews who were here were treated well by us. There was no tension, no rioting and no fighting. Even when we saw shiploads of Jews arriving in the late 19th century and early years of the 20th, we did not resist. We might not have welcomed them warmly but we took them as people of the Book or *Ahl-e-Kitab*. They call our first prophet Abraham, we call him Ibrahim; their biggest prophet was Moses whom we call Musa and respect him. So we were cordial.

It was the Balfour Declaration of 1917 which gave us Arabs a jolt. Britain then was a big imperial power and Prime Minister Lloyd George had blessed the declaration which promised the Jews a homeland, by implication, in the Holy Land. As the 20th century progressed, more and more shiploads of Jews started coming. That is when the tensions started between us and the Jews. In due course, we came to know that they were also importing arms and ammunition. That left us no choice but to get military help from neighbouring Arab countries. After all, Palestine belonged to Arabs who had been in a majority for centuries; it was our homeland. Where else could we go and resettle and why should we? Remember, our Prophet riding Barack the horse, ascended to heaven to meet Allah the Merciful from Jerusalem and returned at the same place in two days' time. That also makes the city one of our holy ones. Until a few decades ago, our namaz used to be read facing Jerusalem. Only recently the *mehrabs* in the mosques point to Mecca. Above all, the whole of Palestine is ours legally by adverse possession for centuries.

Quite accidentally, soon after listening to these Arab gentlemen, I bumped into a Christian couple at the hotel who claimed that their family always belonged to Palestine since 1948 when their parents became Israelis. They said they were happy in Jerusalem which should belong to Christians and not to Muslims just because of the Al Aqsa Mosque which celebrates the Prophet Muhammad's journey to heaven and back. On the other hand, Jesus, the son of God was born at Bethlehem a few miles from Jerusalem. The Lord spent his life around here, preached in Judea and was betrayed and crucified on Calvary Hill. They asked me, "So gentleman you judge if it is an Arab area by right or much more Christian? The Jews are nice to us Christians here".

The several Jews I got to talk to on the subject were clear that they had the first right to Judea. They belonged here before they went to Egypt for employment, but unfortunately the Pharaoh trapped and enslaved them. When Prophet Moses, after years and years liberated us, he brought us back to Judea they said. He was a great soul and wrote the five books of the *Torah*. In fact, there was no Islam in this world until 14 centuries ago whereas the Jewish right to this land is thousands of years old. Jerusalem was founded by us. Our temple on the mount was built by our ancient kings, but demolished by Nebuchadnezzar II of Babylon. We rebuilt it and it was destroyed by another invader. Now only the mount is there on whose Wailing Wall locals as well as visiting Jews pray and often break down and weep.

Please remember, they said, that we have no other country we can call our homeland and go to. We have had to roam all over the world like gypsies since we had no place of our own. Muslims have some 57 countries so they have no problem. Why harass us with bombs and missiles from time to time? At present, it is Hezbollah; tomorrow it could be Hamas and the day after some other group. Palestine should have been reserved for us Israelis. That would have avoided so much of our suffering, anti-Semitism, pogroms and all. It has been nice of us to let others stay in Israel and be happy. Half of Palestine is still theirs. What more Sir? one of them asked.

When I raised the issue of adverse possession they have enjoyed in Palestine for centuries, the answer was ready. You mean that because I stole your grandfather's watch 30 years ago, it is legitimately mine now. You have no right. How would you feel if I did that?

What is happening to Europe?

IN THE SCOTTISH parliamentary election held on 6 May 2021, the Scots voted just slightly less than half in favour of secession from Britain. One wonders what is happening to the continent that gave birth to nationalism as an alternative to monarchy, backed by religion as an ideology to governance. Until 1603 AD, England and Scotland were quite separate states. It so happened that Henry VII's daughter was married to the then King of Scotland and their great grandson was King James VI of Scotland. Elizabeth I, the Virgin Queen, had no possible successor in England. Her nearest relative happened to be the Scottish James VI, Henry VII having been the Queen's grandfather. She approved of him and when she died, James (as James I of England) moved to London and was crowned in 1603. He wished throughout his reign that the two countries be merged under one common monarch but the English nobles did not agree. Eventually, it was in 1707, in the reign of Queen Anne that the merger took place. Now, after over three centuries they seem to be heading for separation.

Since the year 1991, the number of new countries that have asserted their independent way to the map of Europe is almost unbelievable. There have been so many in just a matter of 30 years. The pace was set off by the Soviet Union in 1991 when President Mikhail Gorbachev allowed each federating unit to go its own way. That gesture created 16 countries where only one existed, albeit a few were strictly in Asia. A few years later the two Germanys divided after World War II but became one when Berlin fell due to popular will. Then came the turn of Yugoslavia soon after and it broke into seven countries, namely Serbia, Bosnia, Slovenia, Bosnia-Herzegovina, Macedonia, Montenegro and Croatia. Thereafter, in a few years Czechoslovakia peacefully separated into the Czech Republic and Slovakia to function as separate countries. Until 1918, all these were provinces of the Austro-Hungarian Empire. As a result of the Empire's defeat in World War I, the League of Nations rearranged these nations. News kept filtering that Catalonia or eastern Spain centered around Barcelona wished to secede from Spain.

In contradiction to these many separations, there is also a reverse trend of loose amalgamation that began soon after the end of World War II. One by one, several common communities of several European countries decided to come together under a European Coal and Steel Community, then European Economic Community, then as a Customs Union; in 1967, this EEC and EURATOM (The European Atomic Energy Community) merged. To these six or seven countries, more and more joined like Denmark, Ireland and the UK; soon Spain and Portugal followed. The list kept getting longer.

In 2002, the European Union with a common currency called Euro emerged and around the same time was introduced a common VISA called Schengen. Two general elections to a European Parliament of 20 countries have also been held for the members to sit in sessions at Brussels.

One of the secrets of Europe's success on many fronts through the 18th, 19th and the early 20th centuries was nationalism which was a successor of Christianity as an ideological guide to the rulers. Monarchy and the divine right of the king were not adequate as an ideological aid. Nationalism implicitly demanded an effective government regardless of whether the state was small, medium or large. Unfortunately, leftist or liberal thinkers deliberately confused nationalism with Hitler's Nazism and Mussolini's Fascism and most of the wrong they did. The thinkers' attempt was to damn nationalism in order to make space for communism or its allies to be able to come to power.

Asia and Africa were looked upon as national game as an individual hunter looks upon a wild tiger. This value system gave the European countries considerable initiative and competitiveness. After the end of World War II, these values have been diluted as a result of the amalgamation in the European Union, which is an anti-thesis of nationalism.

If this sounds theoretical, let's take a practical experience. I was visiting Greece to see its ancient sights. A taxi driver complained and said, "We were much happier with our drachma (currency). This Euro has ruined our country. They expect us to be like Germany. Tell me how? We are favourites with tourists and, if required, we can even devalue the drachma. But we cannot because we can do nothing with the Euro. So coming to Greece becomes expensive for tourists. Our leaders who signed the agreement in Brussels thought that we would be rich like Germany!"

On a visit to Paris soon after the EU was a reality, my sister-in-law, who had become a French citizen, complained that prices of everything had shot up; what was in francs was now in Euros. Britain had exited the EC; a country which was a great empire felt stifled under Europe.

Killings in the USA—what they can teach us

KILLINGS IN AMERICA, particularly in shootouts, or murders of citizens by ultra-vigilante policemen, continue. The latest are six victims. Only a few days ago eight persons of Asian origin were killed. The latest incident of societal divide in that country is the conviction of a white police officer, Derek Chauvin, for murdering a black American George Floyd, which triggered off riots under the "Black Lives Matter" movement. The Floyd-Chauvin saga has only further exacerbated the race debate in the USA.

This is not the only incident of its kind. Thirty years ago in 1991, a shocked world saw four white American police officers beating Rodney King, an African American man on his knees, using batons, between 53 and 56 times. The officers were charged with excessive force and assault, but their lawyers argued they could not get "a fair hearing in Los Angeles", so the trial was moved to a conservative county with a higher proportion of white residents—reflected in the makeup of the jury. One lady juror later told the media that she believed King was in "total control" of the event. That juror believed one of the defence lawyers who said, "There's only one person who's in charge of this situation and that's Rodney Glenn King". Thus, the argument went that a Black American man presented a violent threat, even while on his knees and clearly injured.

One needs to diagnose the root cause of the violence. Many blame it on guns being freely available, on former President Trump inflaming inter-racial antagonism or white resentment against coloured leaders coming to power. These are symptoms of a malady which is not merely America's. The history of Europe and the Western world is a long and continual catalogue of war and violence.

Western ethos has been shaped by faiths emanating from the inspiration of Prophet Abraham who, we are told, was asked by God to sacrifice his son Isaac on Mount Sinai. Seeing Abraham's sincerity, the Lord altered his order to sacrificing an animal instead of his son. Nevertheless, the faith was inaugurated with violence. One is a Jew only if one accepts Jehovah as the only God. Christianity proclaims Jesus to be the only son of God, and only those who unwaveringly accept this premise are Christians. Islam says there is no God but Allah. Their holy scriptures–the Torah, Bible and Quran provide authoritative guidance to their followers. If one follows them faithfully, life is good and simple. God sends one to heaven or hell based solely on the follower's adherence to his religion's tenets. It is, therefore, important that one conducts oneself dutifully. Those who do not belong to one's religion are the "Other", whether gentile, heathen or *kafir*. Deviation from the prescribed path is apostasy, which will be severely punished.

Such an ordained way of life commands obedience but there is little scope of any spiritual diversion for the follower. That is the limitation of Deductive Logic, whether a religion or any other system of thought or belief. The given premise is invariable, from which arise corollaries; the follower has only to follow them.

In Indian ethos, based on Hindu or Sanatana dharma, the follower is free to believe or not believe as he likes. There is no insistence on the concept of God. In fact, one can be agnostic and still call oneself a Hindu. The central fundaments most Hindus spontaneously believe in and accept are karma (action) and its effect as *bhagya*. There is freedom of worship, and of pursuit of realisation as to what the universe and its spirit are all about. A Hindu is free to innovate and follow his own path to *mukti* or liberation. In contrast, to please God and hope to get His favourable verdict of going to heaven, there is attraction to fight for one's Abrahamic religion or the community. Jihad or holy wars—Christian crusades and Islamic expansionist wars—mark this way of life.

In other words, Western ethos is on fighting and war. This is the price of lack of opportunity for spiritual freedom. It explains the frequent violence in the West. The concept of the 'Other' whether heathen or *kafir* induces intrinsic hatred. Kingdoms and states in the West and Middle East were founded on the basis of moral certitude, which inevitably led to wars for the propagation of their religious way of life being just. The fraught messianic way of religion, where self-doubt is minimal, increasingly came to colour the modern world of the Abrahamic faiths. Even a cursory look at the West's history reveals the truth of the postulate that much of what we call modernity has been fashioned by the aversion for the 'Other' and conflict.

What is the way out? Renowned English historian Arnold Toynbee perhaps had the answer when he said: "It is already becoming clear that a chapter which had a Western beginning will have to have an Indian ending if it is not to end in self-destruction of the human race. At this supremely dangerous moment in human history, the only way of salvation is the ancient Hindu way. Here we have the attitude and spirit that can make it possible for the human race to grow together into a single family".

India can succeed against China

INDIA'S MISTAKE HAS been to misread China and the character of its leaders. The yellow giant is over 90 percent Han by race, unlike our multilingual culture. China has been a centralised polity for over two thousand years uninterrupted. Mao Zedong, although a Communist, thought of himself as an emperor. He was first a Chinese nationalist and then a Marxist. He had never been to Europe except a solitary visit to Russia. Hence, Mao was dominantly insular, rather like Russia's Josef Stalin. While Jawaharlal Nehru talked of peace and Panchsheel, Mao Zedong believed that political power grows out of the barrel of a gun.

Unlike Indians, the Chinese are intuitively given more to reasoning than to faith. As someone in Hong Kong put it: "We like Confucianism for breakfast, Buddhism for lunch and Taoism for dinner. We are not as god-fearing as you people but we dread losing face, especially to strangers". Jawaharlal Nehru, briefed by Menon, went to the extent of reading the Chinese through the latter's eyes. Indian history was interrupted by the rule of Islamic sultanates from 1206 AD to 1526 and, thereafter, the Mughals took over until 1858, when the Sepoy Rebellion ended. Thereafter, the British Crown formally took over, and Europe influenced Indian thinking for well over 200 years. We Indians are thus cast in several different moulds. On the other hand, as British author and journalist Jasper Becker in his book *The Chinese* has put it, "the Chinese State is probably the oldest functioning organisation in the world, dating back more than 2,000 years". For most of these centuries, it was a centrally-governed empire. It has been dominantly a single race country unlike the diversity in India.

China has never experienced democracy; its people have known only imperial style subjugation. However, all these factors do not make the Chinese invincible. It is necessary to stress this. I still remember the 1962 invasion when I was a resident in Kolkata. The Peking (now Beijing) Radio, twice a day in November of the year, announced that the troops of Peoples Liberation Army, as China's army is called, were looking forward to "celebrating Christmas in Calcutta". The possibility did seem real at the time. When on 21st November we heard on the news at 8 am that the Chinese had declared a unilateral withdrawal, it is difficult to imagine the relief all Indians felt.

Reading through the records of the meetings with Chinese premier Chou En-Lai until 1960, it seems clear that the Chinese wanted us to concede what they had grabbed in Aksai Chin. They wanted to connect Tibet with Sinkiang by a road they had already built. In return, they would concede what we claimed in the eastern and middle sectors. India should give up wanting back the 30,000 square km of Aksai Chin they had occupied in the 1950s, of which Nehru had said in Parliament: "Not a blade of grass grows there". The reality is that no government in Delhi can dare sign off this territory and still hope to remain in power. This may be possible if and when China gets into a corner.

With the most successful of leaders, the wheel of fortune turns and the needle stops and points to misfortune. Adolf Hitler and Nazi Germany could do no wrong between 1933 and most of 1942, a span of nearly ten years. A man, who after four years of World War I could not rise above the rank of corporal, commanded implicit obedience from finest of German Field Marshals. The saga of Napoleon Bonaparte is well known. President Xi Jinping's ambitions are not qualitatively different.

That is when the Quad can come into real play. The USA can provoke Beijing on Taiwan. Japan, with its navy, as well as Australia's can block the appropriate channels of South China Sea. That is when India can play its Himalayan card. India's foreign ministry can and should convince the Russian leadership that the real threat to it will be from China. Russia has vast empty spaces of land in Asia and sooner or later, China is likely to grab some of it. The two neighbours share a long border; Russia has space without people and China has people without space. The two countries fought a war across the Ussuri River in 1969 and there is no reason why they cannot clash again. In 1962, India had the misfortune to be headed by a leader who said that India was a "peace loving country and it did not need an army. The police are sufficient to protect us". Moreover, Nehru's Defence Minister was the communist Krishna Menon who was absolutely certain that China was a 'fraternal' country and could never attack us.

Indian Misreading of China

THE CHINESE ARMY or the PLA (People's Liberation Army) is not a national force but belongs to the Communist Party of China. Its genesis was in first allying with the country's nationalist party the Kuomintang (KMT) led by General Chiang Kai-shek against the Japanese invaders. Thereafter, the PLA fought the KMT in a civil war and defeated them to complete the communist revolution by October 1949. Supposing the Indian army had belonged to the Congress or any other ruling party—would it have become the crack professional force it now is? Moreover, fighting for one's country and obeying a political boss are not the same thing.

Hypothetical outcomes or differences would be seen on the battlefield, if we go deeper into some figures. In 1962, the Chinese invasion was a sorry tale for India. Nearly 5,000 soldiers were killed while about 4,000 were wounded or captured alive. The Chinese admitted that they had lost nearly 750 killed and 1,700 wounded. It is evident that the Indian soldiers, despite being badly clothed and equipped, fought bravely. Else, the Chinese should not have had so many casualties.

During the Korean War in 1951-53, China found the communist North Koreans having to retreat in the face of the overwhelmingly powerful US army aiding South Korea, and went to North Korea's help. By 1953, the PLA had lost an estimated 1,52,000 soldiers killed and 383,000 wounded. In 1967, just five years after its successful 1962 attack on India, China once again tried to grab Indian territory at Nathu La, but was beaten back by the Indian army, suffering 450-500 casualties to just over 70 on the Indian side. In 1979, China decided to invade communist North Vietnam but despite the size of the PLA, it suffered over 60,000 casualties and had to go back in ignominy. Since its 1979 Vietnam misadventure, the PLA has had no combat experience. Its recent attempts at bullying India, first in Doklam and then Ladakh, have met with not only failure but also combat casualties. This history does not speak well of the efficiency of the Chinese army.

In fact, communist militaries are not known to be efficient. Josef Stalin claimed to have played a major role in defeating Hitler's Germany. But such a claim conveniently overlooked the enormity of the Soviet casualties of over 20 million in the four years between 1941-45. Besides, it also ignored the enormous American aid of war material supplied under the Lend-Lease scheme. There is an ideological block with communist militaries; they are unable to develop a proper officer corps. Karl Marx defined the core of his ideology as "from each according to his ability to each according to his need". He forcefully propagated the equality of the entire working class or proletariat as he termed it, but all other classes of people stood excluded from this unity, even peasants. If they had even an acre or two of land, it was collectivised or taken away. Landlords and urban rich were eliminated. Stalin did all this by killing over 30 million Soviet people during his reign that lasted from 1924 to 1953. Coming to militaries, officers must be respected by their soldiers and not be treated as equals. Implicit obedience is essential especially on the battlefield. Communism has destroyed the essence of discipline by prescribing equality. If both soldiers and their commanders are to be political equals as 'comrades', the military or any organisation will fail.

One reason why Communism did not cross the borders of Kerala and West Bengal in India is this bug of equality. It is a contradiction of the Hindu ethos of karma and liberty. One cannot prevent a person from performing better and better karma nor help to boost an individual's poor karma. One of the first steps after 1949 by Mao's regime was to take over the ownership of farming land but, unlike Stalin, it simultaneously leased it back. Communists could not trust any class except those who worked for industries or those dependent on state employment. Ideally, they preferred party service to that of the state. This explains why the army in China is owned by the party.

One may briefly remember what the great leader of Singapore Lee Kuan Yew had said about China in the second volume of his autobiography. "In the next 50 years", Lee said, "the Chinese would have to move from a planned to a market economy, from a rural to an urban base. China's political structures would have to allow its citizens more participation and control over their lives. A third factor would be the widening differences in incomes, growth rates, and quality of life between the wealthy coastal and riverine provinces and the disadvantaged inland provinces. The fourth and most profound factor would be the different values and aspirations of the next generation. Several problems can cause serious disruptions: a breakdown of the banking system, huge unemployment following reforms of state-owned enterprises. However, the most pernicious problem is corruption".

Much of China's economic rise has been export-oriented. Its new factories, small or large, manufacture products that are mostly exported. Many of the larger factories have been set up by foreign entrepreneurs. In such a situation, the country's rulers should ensure friendly relations with all countries, especially the importing ones. But as it happens, the current regime has earned the wrath of most nations of the world. What then would happen to China's exports?

The Role of the Vice-President in India

FORMER VICE PRESIDENT Hamid Ansari's interesting autobiography holds readers' attention. Regrettably, a leader of his stature encouraged the perpetuation of a separate Muslim identity instead of integrating all Indians.

Addressing the students of the National Law School, Bengaluru, Ansari said: "Two obligatory isms: why pluralism and secularism are essential for our democracy. I had argued for an urgency of going beyond tolerance to acceptance, through continuous dialogue for promoting harmony since the need for it is highlighted by enhanced apprehensions of insecurity among segments of our citizen body, particularly Dalits, Muslims and Christians". Once, in an interview to Rajya Sabha TV, Ansari took off on "illiberal nationalism" and "perceptions on Muslims". Yet on a third occasion, he told the Muslim Majlis-e-Mushawarat, "A sense of insecurity is creeping in among Muslims". On the last day of his term in the Rajya Sabha, Prime Minister Modi said, "You will have a feeling of freedom and an opportunity to work, think and talk according to your ideology". Ansari regrets in his book that the prime minister took no note of his performance as the vice president, Rajya Sabha Chairman, diplomat and ambassador.

Our third President Dr Zakir Husain had advised Muslims:

> Our misguided brothers in Pakistan don't realise that if Muslims in Pakistan can wage a war against Hindus in Kashmir why shouldn't Hindus, sooner or later, retaliate against Muslims in India? If the Hindus are not welcome in Pakistan, how can we, in all fairness, expect Muslims to be welcomed in India? Such a policy must inevitably result in the uprooting of Muslims in this country and their migration to Pakistan, whereas it became clear last year, they are no longer welcome, lest their influx should destroy Pakistan's economy. Pakistan is incapable of providing room and livelihood to the 40 million Muslims of India, should they migrate to Pakistan. Yet its policy and actions, if not changed soon, may well produce the result which it dreads. Pakistan claims Kashmir, first, on the ground of the majority of the state's people being Muslims and second, on the ground of the state being essential to its economy and defence. To achieve its objective, it has been threatening to lunch *jihad* against Kashmir in India. We should, therefore, like to impress upon you with all the emphasis at our command that Pakistan's policy towards Kashmir is fraught with the gravest peril to the 40 million Muslims of India.

For harmony and actual integration, the concept of majority/minority should be jettisoned. Advocates of guaranteeing further minority rights in India by supplanting the existing Constitution, if necessary, pretend to overlook broad considerations which distinguish the status of minorities in India from the international problem of minorities in post-War Europe, which have inspired international movements for minority safeguards. In the international sphere, demands for special safeguards to protect the culture or linguistic identity of minority communities emerged from the principle that owing to war, or other circumstances causing territorial changes without the consent of the people residing in those territories, the identity of such communities should be preserved from ethnic extinction by safeguards through international charters and national constitutions.

India's Partition which left behind many Muslims in India took place in the opposite way. The pre-independence Muslim demand led by their leader Jinnah was for a separate homeland for the Muslims who, he asserted, constituted a nation separate from the Hindus. The British rulers conceded to this demand overruling the contention of nationalist Indians that Muslims and Hindus, as well as the other people residing in India, constituted one nation and not two or more. The result of accepting the two-nation theory was the partition of India and the creation of a separate Pakistan. Following this, the Hindu leaders in India could have insisted upon an exchange of population between Pakistan and India, so that all Muslims in undivided India could be transferred to Pakistan. But they did not do so. Those who remained in India did so of their free will. The Partition was the seeking of their own community and not the result of circumstances beyond their control, such as the First or Second World War.

In consonance with the liberal attitude of Hindu leaders, the framers of independent India's Constitution embodied certain safeguards for minorities. But these safeguards were extended to all numerical minorities of all religions, languages and cultures and not to Muslims in particular. Those who opted not to go to Pakistan did so with their eyes open as to the safeguards they might get under the Draft Constitution and not because of any covenant that they would be allowed to demand more and more to serve their sectional interests.

In 1945-46, in the general elections held, the Muslim League had a single point manifesto—Pakistan. There were separate electorates along communal lines in those days. All Muslim League candidates were elected. In short, Muslims voted solidly for Partition regardless of who eventually emigrated or stayed behind. Pakistani historian Hamid Khan may be referred to in his *Constitutional and Political History of Pakistan*.

All these delusions, including those that have crept into the Constitution of India should be credited to Jawaharlal Nehru, who proudly called himself "Muslim by culture and Hindu only by accident of birth".